The Salvation Army and the Cinematograph 1897 – 1929

A Religious Tapestry in Britain and India

by
Tony Fletcher

LOCAL HISTORY PUBLICATIONS
316 GREEN LANE, STREATHAM, LONDON SW16 3AS

Published by
Local History Publications
316 Green Lane
Streatham
London SW16 3AS

© 2015 Tony Fletcher

ISBN 978 1 910722 00 8

All rights reserved. No part of this publication may be reproduced, stored in a retrieval system, or transmitted, in any form, or by any means, electronic, mechanical, photocopying, recording or otherwise, without the prior permission of the publisher and the copyright holders.

Front Cover Illustration
Salvation Army Citadel in Tottenham c1906

Rear Cover Illustration
Two illustrations by Bhil tribesmen of Bramwell Booth's visit to India in 1923

ACKNOWLEDGEMENTS

I would like to thank the following for their help and assistance in the preparation of this book and for permission to use photographs, documents, plans and correspondence in the collections detailed to illustrate this publication.

John Anscombe, John W. Brown, Kathleen Dickson, Bryony Dixon, Alex Gleason, Stephen Grinsted, Janice Healey, Keith Holdaway, Hari Jonkers, Kevin Kelly, Frank Kessler, Marion Kilkenny, Luke McKernan, Ruth McKenzie, Bridget O'Leary, Neil Parsons, Kevin Pooley, Laraine Porter, Emma Sandon, Martin Sheffield, Stephen Spencer, John Sweeney, Gordon Taylor, Karen Thompson, Steve Tollervey, Vanessa Toulmin, Hillel Tryster, David Williams, Salvation Army Heritage Centre, Salvation Army Film and Video Archive, British Film Institute and London Metropolitan Archives.

DEDICATION

This Book is dedicated to
Marion, Aaron, Oisin and Fearghall

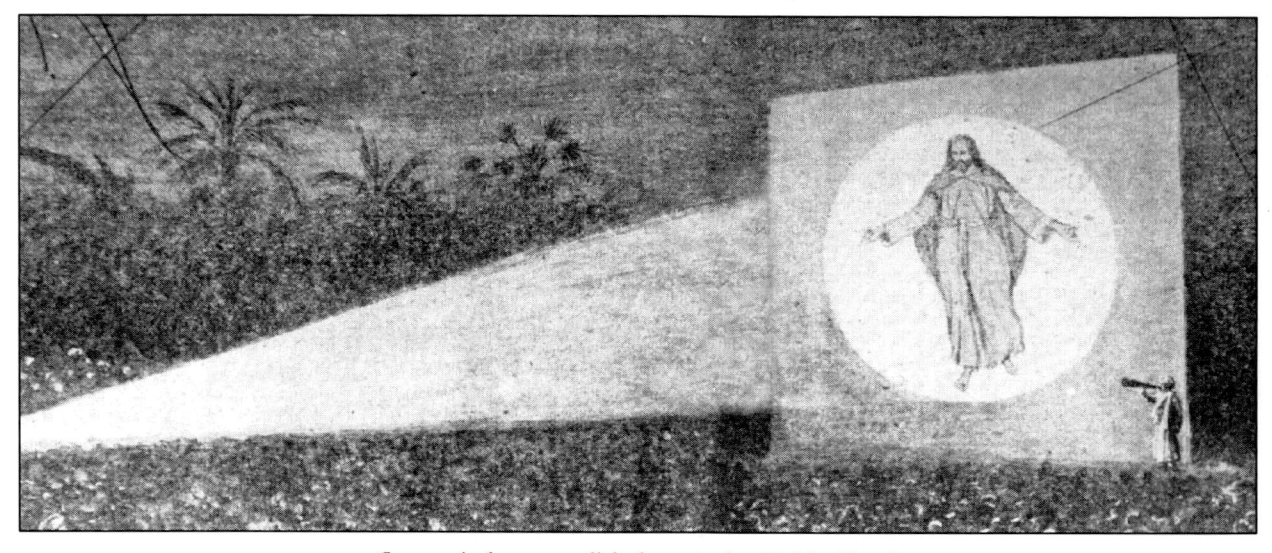

Open-air lantern slide lecture by Fakir Singh

CONTENTS

Introduction 5

Forward 7

Part 1 The First Wave

    The Magic Lantern and the Cinematograph 1891-1902 8

Part 2 Embracing the Cinematograph 1902-1908 26

Part 3 Through India's Coral Strand 59

Postscript 94

Addendum

    Selected films from the Salvation Army's 1906 Catalogue 96

Cinematograph Performances by the Salvation Army

    in India and Ceylon 1906-1919 97

Venues for the 1926/27 Cinematograph Tour in Britain 98

Silent Films from the Pathe and Movietone Archive 99

Main Salvation Army Ranks up to 1930 99

Main Sources 100

'The General' - William Booth

INTRODUCTION

This work investigates the Salvation Army's (S.A.) involvement in utilising film between 1897 and 1929 in order to advance their work and credo in Britain, India, Ceylon, Burma and Java. Their use of film in Australasia has been well documented by Chris Long among other historians.

In Part I and Part II of the book the focus is on the use of the Cinematograph in the British Isles while Part III mainly concerns the social work undertaken by the Salvation Army with the criminal tribes in India. In an endeavour to communicate the work involved in this massive project which they undertook I have recounted, mainly through their own words, what they experienced. The 1925 feature film which the S.A. made on this subject may well have come about after S.A. Officers had viewed Robert Flaherty's film on Nanook and his Iniut family trying to survive in the Arctic – a film which demonstrated that the Cinematograph was not just about entertaining the masses but could also take a serious look at how people lived in other parts of our earth.

I would like to thank Stephen Grinsted and his staff at the Salvation Army Heritage Centre at Denmark Hill, London, where most of my research has been undertaken. In particular, I would like to thank Gordon Taylor who first whetted my interest many years ago when he showed me the Salvation Army Film Catalogue.

Finally I would like to thank John W. Brown of the Streatham Society for his creative input into all aspects of the book.

The Salvation Army Emery Hospital at Anand in Gujerat, India

The Salvation Army Studio.

INTERNATIONAL TRADE HEADQUARTERS,

98, 100 & 102, CLERKENWELL ROAD, LONDON, E.C.

Photography in all its Branches.

Portraiture, Groups, Architectural, etc.

ENLARGEMENTS MADE FROM ANY KIND OF PORTRAIT OR PICTURE.

Portraits of Leading Officers always kept in Stock.

NEGATIVES KEPT.   EXTRA COPIES CAN BE SUPPLIED.

Address all Orders and Applications for Terms to —

The SEGRETARY.

98, 100 & 102, Clerkenwell Road,

London, E.G.

FORWARD

For this book I have compiled the research from a number of conferences papers and talks I have given over the last eight years: - The Domitor Conference at Utrecht (2006); The British Silent Festival at the Broadway, Nottingham (2007); The Visual Delights Conference at Sheffield (2009); The Salvation Army Conference at Regent Hall, Oxford Street, London (2011).

I have presented a number of local history talks including one to the Norwood Society where I looked at the various visual representations that the Salvation Army used in order to disseminate their message including drawings, lithographs, paintings, cartoons, photographs, the Magic Lantern and the Cinematograph. I have tried to incorporate examples from all these aspects in the book.

Most of my research has been undertaken at the Salvation Army Heritage Centre in Denmark Hill. Additional research has been undertaken at The British Library, the London Metropolitan Archives, the British Film Institute Library and the Cinema Museum. The film stills are courtesy of the BFI, the Salvation Army Film and Video Department and the London Metropolitan Archives.

A group of lace makers from the film 'From India's Coral Strand'

PART I
THE FIRST WAVE
THE MAGIC LANTERN AND THE CINEMATOGRAPH 1891-1902

A. Lantern department was opened in 1891 following a Magic Lantern display at the Crystal Palace on the life of Catherine Booth by her youngest son, Herbert. The Lantern department was based at Clerkenwell Road in London. Henry Howse later recalled that he took both portrait photographs as well as manufacturing lantern slides for the Salvation Army. Lantern slide services were given at S.A. Citadels mainly during the winter months between October and April.

In April 1892 an editorial in 'The Field Officer' reported on a lecture by Col. Pearson in Camberwell before two thousand people:– "powerful limelight dissolving views on social branches of our work were shown". The lantern which was used had previously been owned by Prof. Pepper and the un-named lanternist who was said to have travelled with the late missionary Dr. Livingstone to Africa, as his artist and photographer. The editorial stated that fifty to sixty souls were saved "for purity and salvation".

In December 1892 Lt. Henry Howse married Lt. Bessie Palmer at Penge. They both worked at the International Trade HQ which is where the Lantern department was based.

An article in 'The Officer' in March 1893 stated that before Herbert Booth delivered his lecture about his mother the S.A. hierarchy had disagreed about whether they should be using lantern slides, "due to the evils associated with their use". However, they later agreed to change their regulations to adopt the use of the lantern particularly at 'Band of Love Meetings'. The slides had to be approved by the S.A. HQ. It was suggested that an average of forty to fifty slides should be incorporated within each service. There were five headings for the types of slides the S.A. approved of:- 1) S.A. Social and Foreign views, 2) Scriptural subjects, 3) The Life and History of Joseph, 4) Dore's Biblical Pictures and 5) Pilgrim's Progress. Admission to the meetings was 1d. (penny), though admission was free for members of the Band of Love.

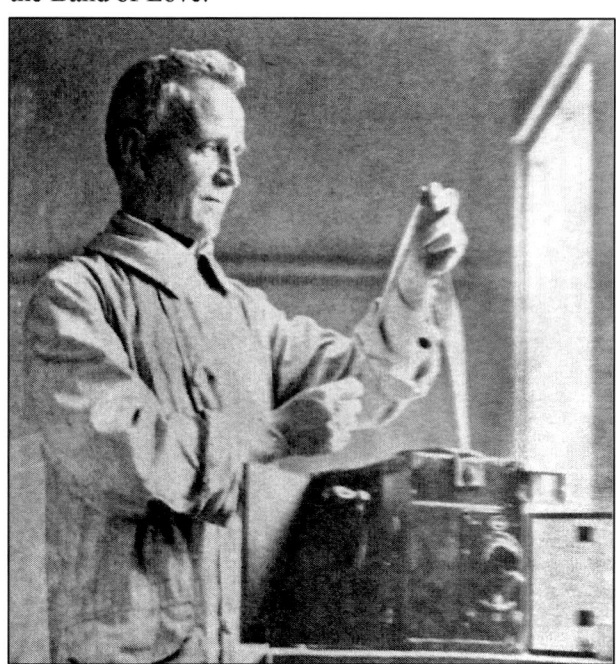

Herbert Booth

Lantern Slide of Catherine Booth

Henry Howse

The S.A. HQ warned that the use of Lantern slides would be prohibited if its use was abused and that it should not become "just a mere exhibition or entertainment for children". The S.A. sold both lanterns and slides at a cheaper price than ordinary commercial manufacturers. In January 1894 there were three types of Magic Lanterns advertised by their "Outfit and Tea department" situated in Clerkenwell Road. The sets being promoted for the winter season 1894-5 included 'The Life of Orange Harriet', 'Sowing the Wind' (or the Story of a Backslider), 'Katie's White Rose', 'A Daughter of Ismael' and 'Fisherman Karl'. 'The Life of Orange Harriet' was sold in two versions:- either thirty plain slides at 33/- (shillings) or twenty eight coloured and eight plain song slides at 50/- .

The Life of Orange Harriet lantern slide

An article in 'The Social Gazette' in February 1895 described a Lantern service held 'in the slums' on the subject of the evils of drink by Major Mildred Duff.

"We stood at the door and watched them come in 'this real Salvation Army sort', we thought with satisfaction as rough-clad men and women, many of them the worse for drink, and wild Jewish-looking girls with ear-rings, fringes and shawls pressed up for 'front seats'. The children had had their share of the treat before, but one little lassie, with pleading face, stood at the door eager for a word with 'Sister'.

'Can mother join the pledge tonight?' she asked. We assured her it was quite possible – a pledge-book is a constant and useful companion of our slum lasses – and she ran away to fetch mother. She presently returned with a decent-looking woman wrapped in a plaid shawl, but smelling woefully of the drink that she had come to sign herself against. We saw the two step up to the front and kept them in mind as the beautiful lantern-slides flashed upon the sheet.

It was a sweet sad story of the 'Life of Orange Harriet' that was told that night to eye and ear, as the gentle voice of the slum secretary told the tale, we felt that, at any rate, to that motley throng, the words went home. It was too dark for us to distinguish their faces, but an influence around told of the eager interest with which they followed. A man who had imbibed just enough drink to make him lively, was highly indignant when the picture of the landlord taking Harriet's grate out for rent was thrown upon the sheet. As to the picture of Little Faith, they were met with almost silence – a true sign in the slum service that each pathetic picture told. When the child was shown singing in the open-air, a captain stood by the lantern and with quiet force, sang the very words of Little Faith's song. 'Say! Will You Meet Me There?' Once, by some mistake, the slide of the child dying was for an instant exposed before its time upon the sheet. 'Oh', exclaimed one woman sitting near us, 'the little girl's bad!' in the horrified voice of one who has just discovered the serious illness of a friend.

Major Duff's talk on the Evils of Drink

It was not by any means a silent audience, but the comments of the 'slummers' told their appreciation of the meaning of the life's story. The narrative which has moved the hearts of many of the 'upper ten' was quite as efficacious to touch the hearts of the very low and degraded. These slummers were quick to catch the drift of each point and the lessons taught so clearly, we feel, must have reached those who, in circumstances so similar to Orange Harriet's, need the same wonder-working power of a great salvation.

When the lights were turned up once more, and Major Duff moved to the front there was no general stampede because the entertainment was over. Only a few went out, while a goodly number remained in the closing meeting, which took the form of a swearing-in. Those warm, enthusiastic soldiers, how our hearts rejoiced over them as they stood with eager hands upon the beloved colours of the Blood and Fire, and swore fidelity to God and the flag. Many of them were getting into uniform, and they were wonderfully respectable looking. But a short time ago, could we have seen some of them, would there have been much of a difference between their appearance and the congregation of roughs and drunkards who had just been looking and listening to the Lantern service? Truly the same power which had changed Orange Harriet had been at work on the people of this particular slum.

But the best finish to the Lantern service in the slums was the prayer meeting. Slum soldiers can pray and believe, and the ejaculations and songs told of the interest that they who had already passed from the bondage of sin took in the souls of those yet enslaved. Slum officers began to move about amongst the people. 'We want to talk to the woman with the plaid shawl. Yes, she had come to 'Join The Pledge' tonight, she said; she had told her husband that she meant to do so. 'I've taken more than is good for one', she said simply. We tried to show her the horror of her sin as well as its consequences, and presently, with firm resolve, she rose to her feet and went to the penitent form. Two drunkards – one the man who had been so indignant about Harriet's grate – were kneeling there too. He whose voice can pierce even through the dull senses of a drink-slave, had not been absent that night; and as the pictures of Harriet's true transformation were thrown upon the screen, he had spoken then and there. Later those who had been kneeling by the side of the seekers rose to the strains of a concertina and with the converts, went off in an exhilarating march down the hall. It was a fitting closing to a beautiful service, and we recognised, as we looked upon the wretchedness and misery of that squalid neighbourhood, the value of such Lantern entertainments. A Lantern service that helps to save souls is the sort suited to the slums – or anywhere else."

A review of "Orange Harriet" in the same issue of 'The Social Gazette' stated:- "Deptford Slummers have had a very beautiful and inspiring visit from Major Duff and Staff Capt. Forward with a Magic Lantern. A lecture on the 'Life of Orange Harriet' was given by Major Duff. Deep and lasting impressions were made. The Meeting was announced outside four pubs and after a grand march and a thoroughly enjoyable time inside, two souls surrendered to God."

The Life of Orange Harriet

During 1896 "Social Slides" were shown as part of the S.A. 'Lantern Rescue Work'. That August the S.A. held an exhibition at the Royal Agricultural Hall in London which included a strand for photography and Rontgen Rays. "Limelight Views" were given at the Berners Hall and "Social Living Pictures" in the transcept. During the exhibition cabinet photographs were sold for 1/- each. In the gallery, the S.A. displayed the Phonograph. However there was no mention of the Cinematograph which had been exhibiting at a number of London venues since February that year.

On 6th February 1897 the S.A. advertised a clearance sale at their business address in Clerkenwell Road. In the tea-room, animated photographs, the Phonograph and X-Rays were shown. The sale was supervised by Lt. Col. Lamb and Brigadier Steward and it was reported that the animated photographs were 'a great hit and should take well throughout the country'.

An article in 'The Officer' stated that during the sale at Clerkenwell, visitors were generally surprised at

THE SALVATION ARMY AND THE CINEMATOGRAPH 1897 - 1929

*A selection of 'social slides' produced by the Salvation Army
including an example from a slide set produced for overseas use (centre)*

THE SALVATION ARMY AND THE CINEMATOGRAPH 1897 - 1929

An outdoor slide show in Little Collins Street, Melbourne, given by the Salvation Army Limelight Department. Screening the 'Rock of Ages' hymn series (28th June 1894)

seeing bills around the building, announcing a show of 'Animated Pictures' - "There the pictures were, moving on the screen as if they were living – the children played so happily on the sea-shore, there the waves came rolling, and further out ships were sailing to and fro.... Adjutant Howse was the 'showman' of the affair ... (he stated that) "the film is reeled through it (the apparatus) very quickly so that about fifteen different photographs are taken every second..... Adjutant Howse thinks that the Frenchman Lumiere can claim to be the first in the market and it is his patent we use .... Unless linked up with the Army, it (ie Animated Pictures) will not get its proper place in Army circles." Howse stated "We have none (S.A. films) for the present but as soon as the fine weather comes, it is our intention to get a series of S.A. pictures. The machine we are making will be able to take photographs as well as show them.... It is our intention to go round the provinces with the machine. Any officer can book us in conjunction with an ordinary Limelight service. The admission will be 3d.; we take two-thirds and leave one-third for the Corps".

Henry Howse later recalled that he had filmed a 75ft. length of film of a group of children paddling in the sea at Brighton, however, the article in 'The Officer' suggests that the film that was shown was made by the Lumiere Brothers and that the S.A. were utilising the Lumiere projector as a camera.

Howse also claimed to have made a film of Queen Victoria's Golden Jubilee Procession in May 1897 with a camera which he himself had built.

In Australia, the Limelight Department was run by Joseph Perry who, at the end of February 1897, purchased a Watson's Motorgraph Cinematograph machine.

The following month he gave a private show of twelve Lumiere

Joseph Perry with his bi-unial projector

12

THE SALVATION ARMY AND THE CINEMATOGRAPH 1897 - 1929

films at the S.A. HQ in Melbourne. During April, Perry went on tour with the Cinematograph which proved to be a success. Herbert Booth who was now in charge of the S.A. in Australasia decided that the Cinematograph should be used in order to illustrate the work that the S.A. undertook and during the summer of 1897 they purchased a Wrench Cinematograph and filmed three local Topicals (ie. news film) in Melbourne.

In May 1897, around the time of Queen Victoria's Jubilee, a Cinematograph fire had occurred in Paris at a charity event when over one hundred people were killed. Although the S.A. in their literature referred to this tragedy they didn't mention the cause until an article appeared in 'The Officer' in 1918 which stated that "a careless operator, refilling a saturator caused the first flame which ignited the films with the loss of hundreds of lives." In September 1897 another serious fire incident occurred in a theatre in St Petersburg when over seven hundred perished.

In November Adjutant Henry Howse wrote a letter to 'The Officer' which stated – "I write to bring before the notice of your readers, our collection of Animated Photographs .... In connection with our Lantern department we have a plant for producing and exhibiting living pictures .... We are open to give exhibitions in conjunction with a good Limelight service at any Corps.... Our terms are as follows – for the London District – one half of the profits with a minimum of £2 guaranteed. We will provide all apparatus including gas".

In January 1898 a Limelight show was given at the Royal Albert Hall, London in the presence of

Cinematograph fire in Paris in May 1897

William Booth just prior to his four month trip to the USA and Canada. The following month Perry gave a Cinematograph demonstration at the S.A. film studios in Melbourne and spent the rest of the year touring with the Cinematograph as well as filming S.A. activities. Among the films he made were "A Hungry Man Stealing Bread and His Arrest by Police", "The Masher's Downfall", "The Thrilling Suicide", and "The Drunken Swell". In July 1898 Herbert Booth gave a lecture entitled 'Social Salvation' which included one hundred slides and six

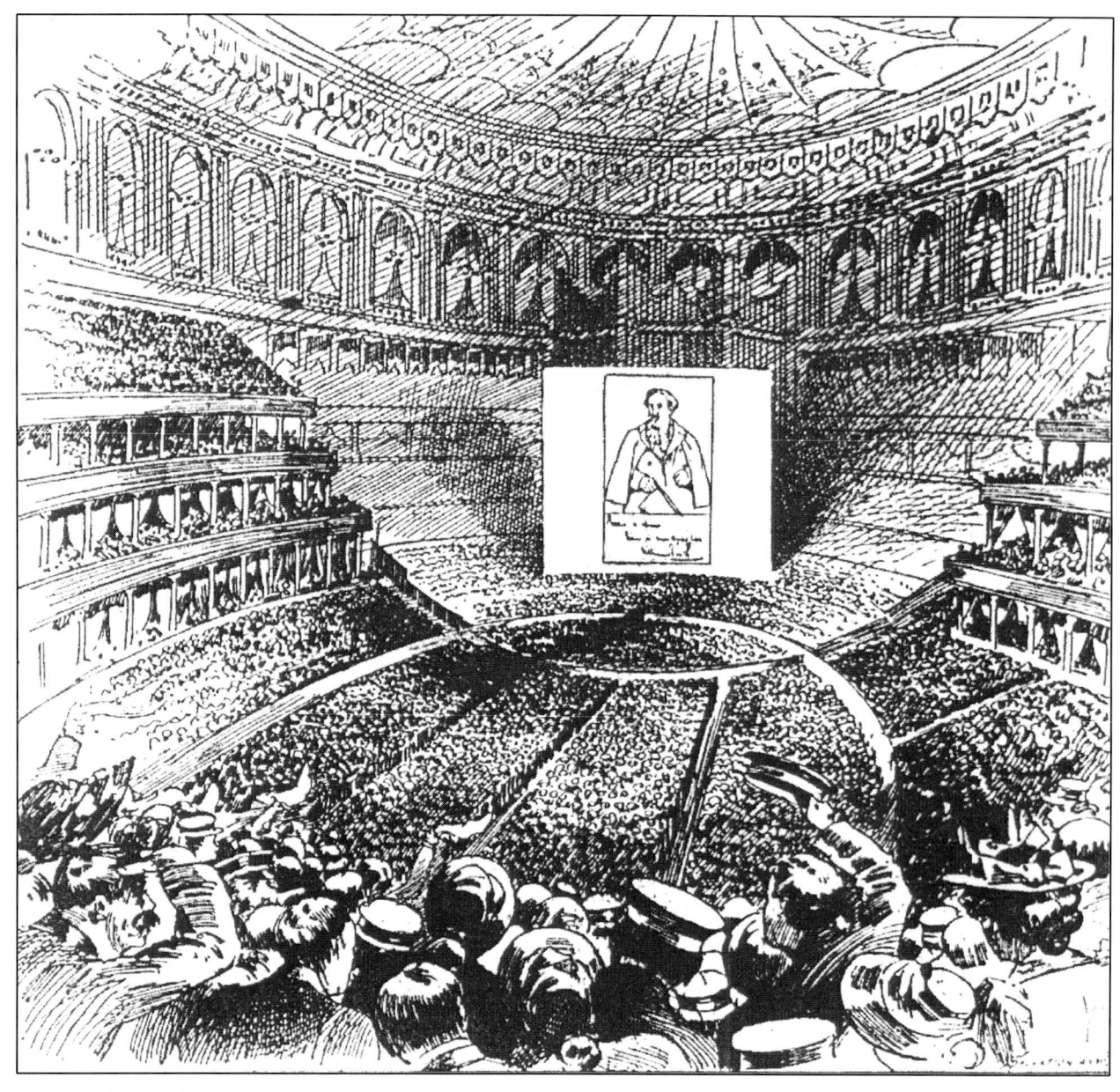

THE SALVATION ARMY AND THE CINEMATOGRAPH 1897 - 1929

The last lantern slide at the The General's farewell at the Royal Albert Hall in January 1898

Cinematograph films. In August 1898 Perry took a film of the S.A. 'Rescue and Maternity Wards'.

In Britain in July 1898 an article entitled 'Salvation Science' appeared in 'The Officer'. It stated that "The Graphaphone, Gramophone, Cinematographe and a host of other phones and graphs had come to stay. In Australia they have been very successful auxiliaries to our work and Mrs Herbert Booth (Cornelie Schoch) is to be congratulated for the way in which she has linked them on to her social lectures... Field Officers should exercise most vigilant care in making them, like the Lantern, a means to an end. We use the train, not to behold the over-varying scenes over which we travel, but to get to a certain destination. The destination, or end, of every meeting, is to get at people's consciences and everything which fails to impress or help in this direction frustrates the business of a Field Officer, no matter how big the crowd he attracts, how substantial the offering, or how pleased the people may be!!"

In the November 1898 issue of 'The Officer' Cinematograph machines of all makes were advertised for sale including the S.A.'s own 'speciality' for £15.

William Booth often began his world tours at the beginning of a new year. In January 1899 he left for a tour of Australasia, his third such visit. He was accompanied by Comm. Pollard, Comm. Lawley and Ensign Barrett. He journeyed first to Paris, then on to Naples, where he continued his journey by boat. Joseph Perry filmed him on a number of occasions on his tour including on February 23rd when William Booth was in quarantine for a week following a smallpox scare on his ship. During this quarantine,

ILLUSTRATED SALVATION STORIES.—No. I.

The Muffin-Man

IT was the Sunday afternoon Open-air. A somewhat beery man, with a basket of muffins on his head, came up and interrupted us. I offered him the ring to say what he had to say. He laid his basket on the ground, but found it easier to interrupt the Army than harangue the crowd. However, he finished by taking up the collection for us. Then, having subdued him by our tact, to the tune of a rattling chorus, we marched him off to the next Open-air stand. We went straight to his own neighbourhood, opened out, formed a ring, and pleaded with him to give his heart to God. I placed my coat on the ground for him to kneel upon. While singing "Rock of Ages," he knelt on a *Social Gazette*, and got blessedly saved. Of course, everybody was jubilant. What about the muffins? The Sergeant-Major distributed them freely to the crowd. Then we marched him, with four or five of his children, off to the Sergeant Major's to tea. When I bade the muffin-man "Good-night," he promised to lead a new life, and he is now doing well.

A. M. N.

I.
A DRUNKEN MUFFIN-MAN APPEARS.

II
IS INTRODUCED TO THE AUDIENCE

III.
IS CONVERTED INTO A COLLECTOR.

'The Muffin Man' A story told in photographs (continued over page)

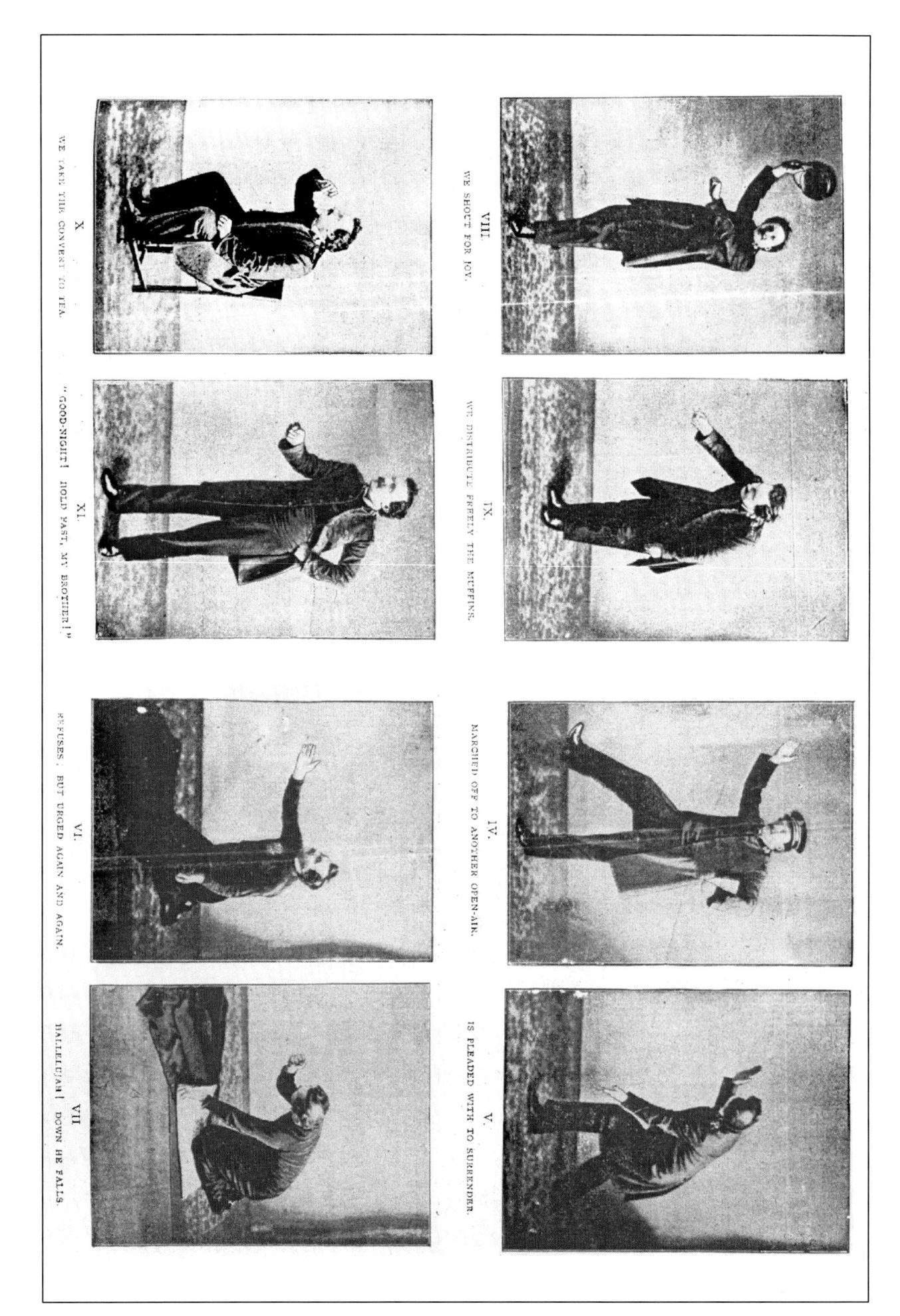

THE SALVATION ARMY AND THE CINEMATOGRAPH 1897 - 1929

VIII.
WE SHOUT FOR JOY.

X.
WE TAKE THE CONVERT TO TEA.

IX.
WE DISTRIBUTE FREELY THE MUFFINS.

XI.
"GOOD-NIGHT! HOLD FAST, MY BROTHER!"

IV.
MARCHED OFF TO ANOTHER OPEN-AIR.

VI.
REFUSES; BUT URGED AGAIN AND AGAIN.

V.
IS PLEADED WITH TO SURRENDER.

VII.
HALLELUJAH! DOWN HE FALLS.

16

Envoy and Mrs Weber and their little daughter

Booth could speak to visitors across a wall. Perry also filmed his departure in May.

In Britain Henry Howse and his assistant Cadet C.W Ollis were transferred at the end of the winter season (ie. end of April 1899) from the Cinematograph and Lantern section of the Trade Department to the Life Assurance Department.

From July 24th to August 8th the S.A. hired the Royal Agricultural Hall in London. The entertainments at King Edward's Hall included the Cinematograph which showed scenes and incidents of the General's recent tour to Australia. Comm. Pollard was in charge of the demonstration.

Joseph Perry had taken five films of William Booth in Australia as follows:

1) In Quarantine in Western Australia at Woodman's Point near Freemantle, where he lived in a small bush hut.
2) His visit to the Bayswater Boys Home in Victoria.
3) His Visit to the Riverview Boys Home in Queensland.
4) His embarkation on SS Arcadia in Largs Bay.
5) SS Arcadia Departing.

Royal Agricultural Hall, London

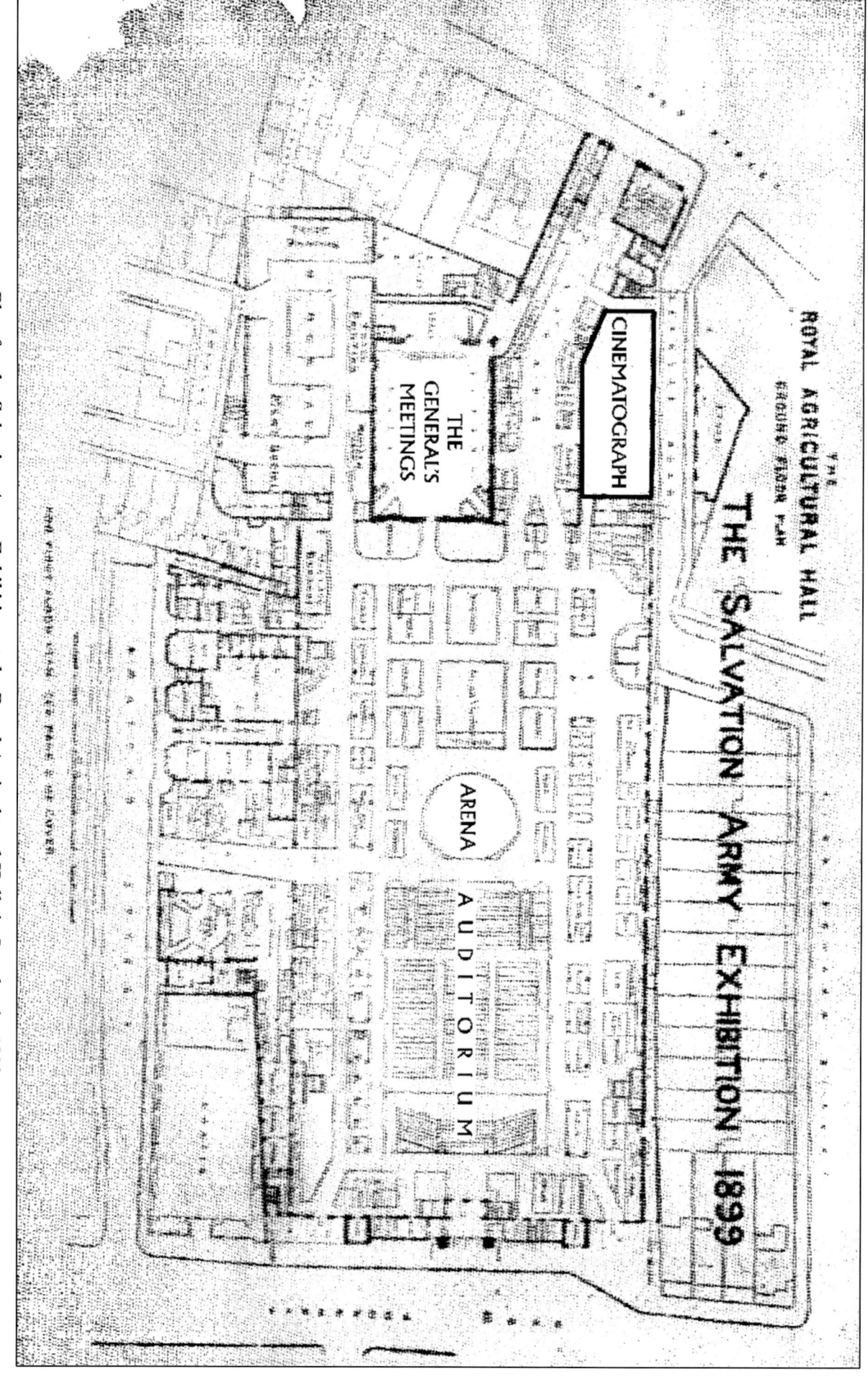

Plan for the Salvation Army Exhibition at the Royal Agricultural Halls in London in 1899

THE SALVATION ARMY AND THE CINEMATOGRAPH 1897 - 1929

THE LANTERN SEASON HAS COMMENCED.

A good Lantern Service, well announced beforehand, rarely fails to draw large crowds; it proves a useful and instructive demonstration. Officers and others are requested to send for our list of Lanterns, Slides, etc., before purchasing elsewhere. READ CAREFULLY THE ANNOUNCEMENT IN CIRCLE.

Special Offer.

First-Class Lanterns, made to our own specification. Japanned Body, Best 4-inch Condensers, and Good Lenses, Four-Wick Lamp, and all the latest improvements.

Worth - - £4 4s.

SELLING FOR A FEW DAYS ONLY

AT

£3 12s.

Special Offer No. 2.

Lantern, after the style of our "International." Supplied complete in Russian Iron Case, at the following very low price:

Advertisement for lantern projectors published in the 'War Cry' 21st October 1899

The Anglo-Boer War (also known as The South African War) began on September 8th of that year, 1899. In March 1900 an article appeared in 'Assurance' from the editor following the Relief of Kimberley (on Feb 17th). The article stated that Henry Howse, who worked in the same office, had received a phonecall from his wife in Penge advising him that his brother Reuben had written from Natal where he was with the British Army. Howse's other brother was also in South Africa and had written to him on Feb 10th from the Orange River stating how important it was to receive letters on a daily basis. That month Howse published an article on the Hecktograph.

A LESSON OF THE WEEK.

PRAY, THAT WARS MAY CEASE !

Published in the 'Social Gazette' 28th July 1900

Meanwhile in Australia, Perry had acquired a second Lumiere camera and now had three operators to assist him. Instead of filming just S.A. activities, they had agreed to accept commissions from outside organisations. This included filming a contingent of Australian soldiers leaving for South Africa. In September 1900 Herbert Booth gave the premiere of 'Soldiers of The Cross'. This was a two-hour lecture which incorporated film with slides. Herbert's wife, Cornelie Schoch took over as lecturer when Herbert became ill. By the end of November he had reorganised his 'Social Work' lecture, adding new film segments and re-naming it 'The Austral Underworld'. Joseph Perry gave a trial tour that month with the newly formed 'Biorama Company', which now had five musicians in addition to lecturers and projectionists.

They were also commissioned to make a film of the inauguration of the Australian Commonwealth.

Meanwhile in Java, S.A. missionaries had given a Limelight and Kinematograph exhibition at the end of 1900.

In May and June 1901 the Duke and Duchess of York, who later became King George V and Queen Alexandria, visited Australia and New Zealand and this event was filmed by the S.A.

Herbert Booth was still on sick leave, having it seems suffered some form of breakdown. In February 1902 he resigned his commission in the S.A.

Herbert wrote to his father, William, and to his eldest brother, Bramwell, with a request that he might purchase the Cinematograph equipment, films and slides which he had been responsible for. It took three years for this matter to be concluded during which time Herbert had joined his sister, Emma, in the USA, where she was in charge of the S.A. activities there along with her husband, Frederick Booth-Tucker. By the end of 1902 Herbert was exhibiting 'The Struggle of the Early Christians' in the USA.

In Australia, Joseph Perry had put together a film slide entertainment entitled 'Under the Southern Skies' which incorporated thirty five film segments along with two hundreds slides. The presentation lasted about two hours.

In October 1902, William Booth left for a visit to the USA and Canada. A record was taken of this visit by an unnamed camera operator using both Lantern slides and the Cinematograph.

In 'The War Cry' in October 1902 an illustration appeared of a Mutoscope exhibition. The accompanying article referred to the exhibition which had been held fourteen months earlier (about Aug 1901). The article went on to state that Mr. Cane, an MP in the House of Commons, had called the House's attention "to the mischievous and demoralising influences of Mutoscope exhibitions". He called them "abominations" and stated that the number of exhibitions being given had decreased due to the press coverage over the issue. Cane stated that instead of exhibiting obscene and degrading pictures large numbers of views relating to ceremonies and processions had been introduced into the Mutoscope exhibitions.

The decision by the S.A. in Britain to distance itself from the Cinematograph between the years 1898 and

A Story in Shadows.

1. Jones frequents the public-house. He goes forth in a state of mad drunkenness.

2. He reels home, meets his little girl, and shamefully ill-treats and kicks her.

3. The police are called and Jones is taken to jail.

4. In jail he is visited by the "War Cry" Sergeant, who talks and prays with him, finally leaving a "War Cry."

5. On his release he seeks The Army, and makes up his mind to give his heart to God.

6. He is now a respectable man and a Soldier of the corps. There is some rumour that he will be made Pub Sergeant-Major.

An example of Shadowgraphy

THE SALVATION ARMY AND THE CINEMATOGRAPH 1897 - 1929

'The Social Mutoscope - Admission Free!'

1902 may have come about due to two significant factors: a) the fire at the Bazaar de La Charite in Paris, and b) the regulations brought in by the London County Council in 1898/9 to first ensure that a suitable barrier must be arranged around the Cinematograph. Later a requirement to have an iron enclosure for the Cinematograph was deemed necessary. The S.A films that were taken during this period do not seem to have been included in their 1906 Catalogue, however, several may have survived. There is a film of three of the children of Bramwell Booth and his wife, Florence Soper, which were probably taken in the late 1890's. Another film which survives is of an S.A. meeting outside a public house. This is on a 17.5mm guage and was filmed by a Biokam camera which was marketed for home use by the Warwick Trading Company about 1899. There is also a somewhat puzzling film of William Booth being handed some food over a fence. This may possibly be a re-creation of his quarantine in Australia.

A slum scene in St. Mary's Hall

During William Booth's visit to the USA and Canada in 1902, he had met up with his two daughters Emma and Eva, who were respectively in charge of each of these territories. He was accompanied by Comm. Lawley and Frederick Cox, who was his aide-de-camp. On their return, a reception was given for William at the Royal Albert Hall which included a "Grand Cinematograph and Lantern Display illustrating his trip including principal scenes of the General's glorious campaign – 'Crossing the Ocean, we sailed up and down New York harbour, entered the great cities of the Commonwealth, sat in the Senate, talked with the President, crossed the Rockies and came back to London Town, all the realities of the desperate fight still before us."

'Devouring pictures of a questionable character'

A story told in pictures from 'The Deliverer' December 1899

THE SALVATION ARMY AND THE CINEMATOGRAPH 1897 - 1929

WORK BY WOMEN FOR WOMEN.
See page 181.

"THE CALL OF THE HOLY ONE."
See page 188.

The Deliverer

Vol. XII.—No. 11.]　　　　LONDON: MAY, 1901.　　　　[ONE PENNY. POST FREE, 1s. 6d. PER ANNUM.

THE AUTOBIOGRAPHY OF BLACK-HAIRED LUCY.　　*[See next page.*

An illustrated story from 'The Deliverer' May 1901

THE SALVATION ARMY AND THE CINEMATOGRAPH 1897 - 1929

An illustrated story from 'The Deliverer' May 1902

PART II
EMBRACING THE CINEMATOGRAPH 1902 – 1908

A Wrench cinematograph projector ready for action

During May 1903 several rehearsals of Living Pictures were given for Bramwell Booth. One was held on Saturday 9th May at Clapton and another on Sat 16th May. In Bramwell Booth's events diary for Wednesday 27th May it states that during an interview with Comm. Coombs, Bramwell Booth had decided on how the S.A. should use the Cinematograph. He stated that worldly or Godless subjects should be avoided and selected six subject headings as follows:

1) To represent the work of the S.A.

2) To illustrate S.A. songs

3) Natural History subjects including animals mentioned in the bible

4) Travel subjects

5) Views of Britain including London and London life

6) Historical subjects such as martyrdom

On June 18th Bramwell Booth attended a twenty minute rehearsal of the proposed Cinematograph display in the Trade department at International HQ. They had been filmed at 15fps and were developed by Howse and Cox themselves. They included one fiction episode which was filmed on the River Lea, however, most of the films were Topicals and

Crowds attend the cinematograph show at a Salvation Army Citadel in Tottenham, London, c1906

PALACE GARDEN HALL,
NUNEATON.
FRIDAY, SATURDAY, SUNDAY, and MONDAY, JANUARY 1st, 2nd, 3rd, & 4th, 1904.

Week Nights at 8 o'clock; Sunday at 6-45   FOUR NIGHTS ONLY.

THE ARMY'S
.. OWN ..
Cinematograph Exhibition

A MARVELLOUS MANIFESTATION OF **ANIMATED PHOTOGRAPHY.**

THE TREAT OF A LIFETIME!

Produced by the **SALVATION ARMY** at enormous expense.

The Exhibition includes the following subjects:

SCENES AT THE LAND COLONY, HADLEIGH.
The Colonists at Work Poultry Farming, Brick-making.

A TRIP ROUND THE LONDON ZOOLOGICAL GARDENS
The Rhinoceros in his Den.   Monkeys at Play.   Lions Feeding.
Tigers and Leopards.

PHYSICAL DRILL by SCOTTISH CHILDREN. Life-like Evolutions

OUR SLUMMERS AT WORK.
An Open-air Scene. A Fight— The Policeman -The Capture.

OUR SLUMMERS AT PLAY.
The Trip Playing in the Fields— Return Home.

THE ILLUSTRIOUS LIVING. OUR HONOURED DEAD.

LONDON STREET SCENES.
The Busy Thoroughfares - Endless Traffic London Bridge with its teeming life, and other noted places.

ANIMALS AT HOME.

HIGH-CLASS DISSOLVING VIEWS
And many other Animated Pictures of special interest.

Lecturer - - MAJOR COX , Operator - ADJUTANT HOWSE
(SPECIALISTS FROM LONDON).

Admission: Reserved Seats, 1s.; Select Seats, 6d.; Back Seats, 3d.
Children under 12 Half-price. Children's Exhibition at 6 o'clock, Admission 2d.

STAFFORD & Co., Typ., Netherfield, Notts.

Leaflet for a cinematograph show at the Palace Garden Hall in Nuneaton in 1904

May 1903

Wednesday 27th

165

The Chief in the Office at 10.30. He saw during the day Comm. Nicol; Mr. S.L. Cooper of Cardiff; Colonel Thur. Cooper on their departure for Finland; Colonel Rach.; Colonel Wilson; Adjutant Christian & Captain Tritton in reference to Sweden Work; Comm. Coombs; Major Cort; Colonel Park.

At Comm. Coombs interview the Chief gave the following decisions in regard to the use of the Cinematograph in the Army.

(a) We can do anything with it which represents the Army but not which illustrates Salvation.

(b)   ditto   Songs

(c)   ditto   Natural History — especially animals mentioned in the Bible — the raven, scorpion, ant

---

May 1903

166

bee, locust, etc.

(d) ditto Geography — Cities travels.

(e) Views in the country, not only in ships, but also — the instruction of London — and London life.

(f) Historical — that is handy pts. Flint Severs — Roads. Hard cases to be taken not to introduce what is unlikely or Godless.

The Chief expressed a wish that the harsh Military display should be avoided.

At the same interview the Chief decides that the Staff Council should take place in September, the

Mr. Cooper informed the Chief that his Bureau desire is to place a

---

Bramwell Booth Events Diary for May 1903

THE SALVATION ARMY AND THE CINEMATOGRAPH 1897 - 1929

interest subjects eg. A Visit to London Zoo, Cinematograph views from the top of St. Paul's, A Train approaching, The S.A. Farm Colony at Hadleigh in Essex, S.A. Juniors Drilling and an S.A. Open-air Meeting in Whitechapel Road.

Most of the films were about 150ft each (ie. 2 -3 mins in duration) and were scheduled to go on tour around Britain accompanied by a string band from Brixton Corps. The object of the tour was to convert the sinner. The S.A. considered that there were two paths into the Soul – "Through the ear and through the eye".

At Southend fifteen people professed salvation over a weekend. Altogether sixteen meetings were conducted in London and the Eastern Counties and although admission was not free, large crowds attended and in all, seventy souls professed salvation.

One report stated that "the first picture was an S.A. open-air meeting in Whitechapel Road, and outside a stream of traffic passed across the screen; we almost imagined ourselves looking on the scene from a first floor window." S.A. Citadels that were visited included Canning Town, King's Lynn, Norwich, Sherringham, Yarmouth, Lowestoft, Diss, Leyton, Stratford, Barking, Poplar, Waltham Abbey, Manor Park, Edmonton and Burnham-on-Crouch.

The tour continued early in 1904 with Cox and Howse visiting the English Midlands, while Brig. and Mrs. Noyce toured Ireland with a second Cinematograph machine.

While this was happening in Britain, an event took place in the

Top: Emma Booth-Tucker's funeral in new York 1st November 1903
Centre: General and Mrs Osborn and Commissioner Edward J Parker (right) at the grave of Consul Emma Booth-Tucker in the Army plot at Kenisco Cemetery 19th June 1948
Bottom: Edward Justus Parker

USA which caused shock waves to the Booth family – Emma had died following an accident sustained in a train crash. Her last public meeting had taken place in New York at the Miner's Theatre on the Bowery on Sunday October 4th 1903. The following Thursday evening she started her tour of the 'West'. On Wednesday October 28th at 3.30am the train she was travelling in was approaching the depot at Dean Lake, Missouri, when it crashed. The passenger coaches were derailed and thrown against a large steel water tank. She had been travelling in the front coach and was seriously injured. She died two and a half hours later, the only fatality from the crash.

On November 1st, on Sunday afternoon, a funeral service was held at the Carnegie Music Hall and on the following day, a further service was held at the Memorial Hall. On Tuesday November 3rd she was buried at Woodlawn Cemetery where two of her own deceased children, William and Evangeline, were buried.

The funeral was filmed by Edward Justus Parker, who ran the Lantern department for the S.A. in the USA. Parker had started his working life as a reporter on a provincial newspaper and he claimed that this was his first attempt at film-making. He printed and developed the film himself. The film survives as part of the S.A.'s own film production 'William Booth, God's Soldier'.

During 1904 Parker developed a lecture entitled 'The Problems of the Poor' which incorporated

29

Train crash at Dean Lake, Missouri, in which Emma Booth-Tucker died on 28th October 1903

THE SALVATION ARMY AND THE CINEMATOGRAPH 1897 - 1929

both Cinematograph film and Lantern Slides. Parker also designed a Stereoptikon as well as the 'Warrior' Camera.

In Bramwell Booth's events diary for December 1903 there is a reference to a financial settlement involving his brother Herbert, which included transferring the Cinematograph account from Melbourne to International HQ. It seems that if Herbert agreed to pay the outstanding balance due by January 1st 1905, then the S.A. would deduct 25% of what was owed.

The British tours by Frederick Cox and Henry Howse continued until early March 1904. They visited Nuneaton, Birmingham, Walsall, Wolverhampton, Crewe, Longton, Coatbridge, Hanley, Newcastle, Swadlincote, Attercliffe, Sheffield, Inverness, Thurso, Kirkwall and Wick. At the Palace Garden Hall, Nuneaton, coloured dissolving views representing scenes from the life of Christ were shown by Limelight. This held the crowd silently spellbound and fourteen souls came to kneel at the mercy-seat. Performances were given between the Friday and Monday of January 1st – 4th at 8pm (apart from Sunday when it was at 6.45pm). The films advertised in the surviving handbill were as follows:-

Scenes of childhood poverty in the early 1900s

1) Scenes at the Land Colony, Hadley – the colonists at work – poultry farming – brickmaking.

2) A Trip Round the London Zoological Gardens – the rhinoceros in the den – monkeys at play – lions feeding – tigers and leopards.

3) Physical Drill by Scottish Children – life-like evolutions.

4) Our Slummers at Work – an open-air scene – a fight – the policeman –the capture.

5) Our Slummers at Play – the trip – playing in the fields – return home.

6) London Street Scenes – the busy thoroughfares – endless traffic – London Bridge with its teeming life and other noted places.

7) Animals at Home.

8) The Illustrious Living. Our Honoured Dead.

9) High class dissolving Views and many other Animated Pictures of Special Interest.

The lecturer was advertised as Major Cox and the operator Adjutant Howse. Prices for admission were 1/- for reserved seats, 6d. for selected seats, 3d. for back seats; children under 12yrs were half-price. At 6pm a children's exhibition was given where admission was 2d.

31

A Day in the Country for the Slum Children—An Appeal.

THE SLUM CHILD'S DREAM—A DAY IN DAISY-LAND.
A Shilling from You will Make the Dream a Reality.

The Contrasting Life of Two Sisters

During this same period Brig. and Mrs Noyce visited S.A. Citadels at Lisburn, Portadown, Newry, Bainbridge, Londonderry, Limavaddy, Coleraine, Portrush, Ballymena, Belfast, Ballymacarat, Holyrood, Inverurie, Peterhead, Frazerboro, Woodside, Brechin, Milsborough, Thornaby, Stockton, Hartlepool, Darlington, Spennymoor, Bishop Aukland, Witton Park and Abitellery. Other venues where the Cinematograph was shown included Warrington, Congress Hall in Clapton and Highgate. A Cinematograph was also brought on tour to Sweden by Comm. William McAlonan.

An article in the Australian edition of the 'War Cry' for Saturday March 5th 1904 featured 'The War Mutoscope' – 'The frontispiece shows the world agog crowding around a war Mutoscope, while his satanic majesty kindly turns the handle of the machine. What does the world behold? – A fascinating scene – two nations engrossed in a deadly conflict, both intent upon the sacrifice of blood and treasure to gain supremacy. A pitiable spectacle at the beginning of the 20th century. The world is truly agog, that is, filled with the desire to witness the deadly combat.' This seems to have been a reference to the Russo/Japanese war which was taking place at the time.

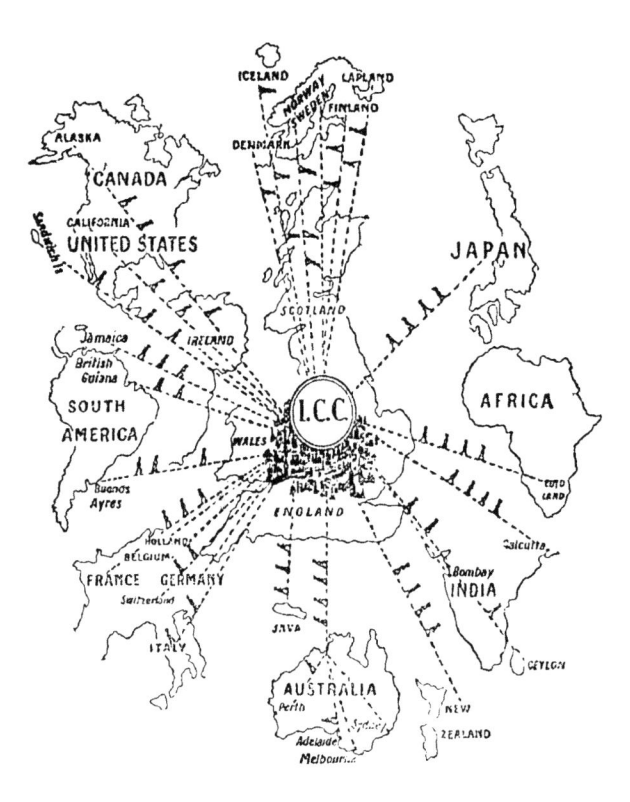

'All lines lead to the great International Congress with contingents of Salvationists in Australia, India, and Japan will soon be embarking for England.'
'War Cry' 2nd April 1904

Plans were being prepared for an International Congress to be held in London in June and July 1904. It was announced that Joseph Perry and Staff Captain Dutton would head the Biorama Company as part of the Australian contingent. They brought with them an orchestra consisting of a piano, violin, trombone, bass viol, side drum, castanets, cornet, triangle and cymbals.

From June 24th to July 8th delegates from forty nine countries attended the International Congress which included a specially constructed reception hall in The Strand on a site which had previously been occupied by the Globe Theatre and the Opera Comique.

International Congress Hall in the Strand 1904

THE SALVATION ARMY AND THE CINEMATOGRAPH 1897 - 1929

Perry gave a Biorama performance at 9.30 am. on July 5th 1904, at the Theatre at the Crystal Palace in Sydenham. One film shown depicted an episode entitled 'Attack of Aborigines on Settlers and their subsequent rout by a Policeman'. Perry operated the films and the lecturer was Lt. Col. Gilmour. Other films shown depicted their social work, views of land and water, the Prison Gate Brigade at work, the sea shore at Manley, a fishing fleet and 'Outward and Homeward Bound'.

Joseph Perry had also filmed events at the Congress and he showed these at the Crystal Palace. They included the foreign contingents arriving at Clapton, holding Meetings, marching through the streets and fraternising. Film of the International Hall in The Strand was shown as well as William Booth starting off on one of his campaigns. Other films that Perry shot while in Britain included London Slum scenes and Abney Park Cemetery where Thomas McKie, who headed the Australian contingent, visited the grave of Catherine Booth. On their return journey to Australia, the party visited several European cities and Perry filmed scenes in Berlin, Frankfurt, Amsterdam as well as in Sweden. He also gave Cinematograph displays in both Amsterdam and Berlin.

Henry Howse had also filmed a number of events at the Congress. The 1906 S.A. Catalogue lists twenty three films from the Congress totalling 3095ft.

1) The General and Staff leaving Strand hall.

2) Foreign Contingents (in 2 parts).

3) German Contingents and Negro Children.

4) Joe the Turk and Chinese Officers.

5) Japanese, Negroes and Dances.

6) Bermuda Band and Indian War Dance.

7) Reception of members of the Congress.

8) Comm. McKie with Indian Boys and Finns.

9) The Junior Encampment with the General.

10) Visit of Representative Congress Group to Clapton (4 sections)

The General taking the salute at the Crystal Palace

THE SALVATION ARMY AND THE CINEMATOGRAPH 1897 - 1929

THE WAR CRY, July 20, 1907.

LONDON'S CELEBRATION OF THE ARMY'S 42nd ANNIVERSARY.

THE WAR CRY

OFFICIAL GAZETTE OF THE SALVATION ARMY.

INTERNATIONAL HEADQUARTERS. [Registered at the General Post Office as a Newspaper.] QUEEN VICTORIA STREET.

No. 1,617.]   LONDON, SATURDAY, JULY 20, 1907.   [PRICE ONE PENNY.

The General Leaves from the Crystal Palace on his Fourth Great Motor Campaign.

THE SALVATION ARMY AND THE CINEMATOGRAPH 1897 - 1929

THE TORCHLIGHT PROCESSION SEEN FROM THE TERRACES OF THE CRYSTAL PALACE.

11) The British Staff at Clapton

12) Crystal Palace Band Parade

13) Crystal Palace Grounds

14) March Past at Crystal Palace (3 sections)

15) Open-air Band Festival

16) The Salvation Negro

17) Negro Officers

18) Foreign S.A. contingents at Clapton

19) International Congress Hall London

20) Arrival of American S.A. Contingents at Clapton

21) Seventy Thousand People at the Crystal Palace

22) European Tour Scenes

23) Grand March past General Booth by Salvationists.

A number of these scenes survive in the S.A. film which was made by Hugh Baddeley from Archive material around 1955.

Prior to leaving London on August 12th to return to Australia, Perry filmed the 75yr. old William Booth departing on his first Motor Car Ministry Tour. William Booth had set out on the first of a series of seven annual motor campaigns around Britain. He now considered himself to be an itinerant evangelist and believed the automobile was the best means of transport to reach outlying towns and hamlets where the railway did not always reach. Over a seventy nine day period from August 9th he travelled 1,224 miles holding one hundred and sixty four Meetings including seventy four indoor rallies. There were five motor cars which started out from St. Just in Cornwall with the final destination being Aberdeen. It seems that only the final section of this pilgrimage, when he visited Scotland between September 2nd and 6th was filmed: from Aberdeen to Montrose, Brechin, Forfar, Arbroath, Dundee and villages and towns in between.

The General starts from Penzance to Land's End where the great motor campaign began

Louis Wain comic strip based on the General's motor campaign published in the 'War Cry' December 1901

THE SALVATION ARMY AND THE CINEMATOGRAPH 1897 - 1929

The Gaumont Company issued a film from the motor tour in their catalogue. It was called 'Pictures of General Booth's Great Motor Tour' with a subheading, General Booth Preaching (in 2 parts).

It was described as follows:

"Gen. Booth's Great Motor Tour from St. Just (Land's End) to Aberdeen, terminated on 6th September, with his arrival the Granite City and reception by Lord Provost and the City Council, also countless enthusiastic admirers, many of whom had travelled a great distance to take part in the General's reception.

The tour was in every way a great success and the idea of 'Evangelism by Motor' was in itself so strikingly original that everywhere the General was welcomed by a vast crowds, and was 'feted' and honoured by the dignitaries of every town through which he and his followers passed. The welcome of the villagers was no less striking or sincere, and the venerable Chief of the S.A. has now the satisfaction of knowing that in addition to having made thousands of new friends, he has cemented old ties, and has in many cases, erased misconceptions respecting the great work of which he has been 'the man at the wheel' for so many years.

Our operator was fortunate in securing on the very last day of the Great Tour, a picture which illustrates, in a remarkable manner, the kind of welcome accorded the General in the towns and villages passed on the way.

Part 1: At Montrose – The picture opens with a view of the crowd waiting outside the Burgh Hall, Montrose, many close portraits of characteristic Scottish types being secured. We then see the cars dash up – and very prominent is the ticketed 'General's Car', which halts right in the forefront of the picture. The General stands up, waves his arms in welcome to the crowd and then alights, assisted by his son, Mr. Bramwell Booth. The Provost is waiting to receive them, and after salutations have been exchanged the party walk off right past the camera, exceedingly close and lifelike portraits being obtained.

Part 2: At Bervie (Kincardineshire) A small and bleak coast village some miles south of Aberdeen. The humble villagers are grouped around the old 'Market Cross' awaiting with eager expectancy, the General's arrival, the children, with hymn-books in hand, are ready to give him a most appropriate welcome by singing 'Onward Christian Soldiers'. Soon the cars dash up, and the crowd gathers round. After a brief breathing space, General Booth stands up to address the assembly. What a sight it is! Here is the patriarchal evangelist, with his snowy white hair glistening in the sunlight, expounding the old truths to the humble villagers, who listen with the greatest interest. So close and striking is the portrait of the General, that one can see at a glance when he is driving home any remarks of great import. The manner of his delivery, which is of the vigorous type, is a study. The picture closes with the General calling upon his son to pronounce benediction, which he rises to do."

38

During December 1904 a film of the General's motor tour was shown at the Congress Hall, Clapton to an audience of 1,500, which included local lads from Homerton in East London who referred to the projector as the 'sinney maty graff'! A further Cinematograph show of the motor tour was given at the Marylebone Hall.

During the 1904 Congress some reorganisation of the S.A. had taken place. Eva Booth had been transferred from Canada to take charge of the USA following the death of her sister Emma. Emma's widower Frederick Booth-Tucker returned from the USA on November 17th with his six children in order to become the new Foreign Secretary of the S.A. in place of Comm. Howard who had retired. Booth-Tucker took over the responsibility and care of 14,000 Officers in forty nine countries.

In an article, Henry Howse had suggested that Field Officers should not attempt to purchase films themselves since it would not be cost effective. However, he did encourage local Officers to purchase Cinematograph Projectors. For a Divisional Officer overseeing twenty Corps, Howse considered that the purchase of films would be cost effective, since after forty viewings the film would have covered its cost; after which they could be exchanged for others. Howse stated that film should always be interspersed with slides which related to the films being shown. He thought that between 1500 – 2000ft of film plus fifty to sixty slides would be a guide for a ninety minute presentation. An entry charge of 3d. and 6d. should be requested. He considered that a Cinematograph exhibition should never be a "Penny show". Howse and Cox did not repeat their Cinematograph tour of the winter of 1903/4 since Frederick Cox had been transferred to work again as William Booth's personal assistant. . It seems that Howse may have returned to managing the Cinematograph and Lantern department.

Popular Saturday Nights or PSN's as they were called, became the vogue at a number of Citadels during the winter nights of 1904/5 where the 'Cineo' was the featured attraction. Among these venues were Glasgow City Hall, as well as three London Citadels – Wood Green, Willesden Green and Congress Hall, Clapton. At Glasgow City Hall one programme of service included fourteen items as follows:

1) Illustrated Song 'Wonderful Words of Life' (sung by the congregation)

2) Prayer (one person)

3) Life-model Subject –'The Ringing of the Bell' – 'Story of a wife's Heroism in seeing the crew of a burning Vessel

4) Illustrated Song 'Eternal Father' (all audience)

5) Cinematograph 'Outdoor Recreations in Canada in Winter' (Snowshoe walking and skating)

6) Swimming and Diving

7) Illustrated Song 'Pull for the Shore' (whole congregation)

8) Cinematograph 'Life and Scenery in Borneo'

9) Smugglers Captured while at Work (moral applied 'Be Sure your sins will find you out')

10) Interval of 10 minutes (War Cries; Young Soldiers; Social Gazettes) Buns and Chocolates on sale

11) Band Selection

12) Illustrated Song (Solved by Officer's Daughter)

13) Life-Model Subject 'Not Wanted' (The story of a Crippled self-sacrifice)

14) The Cinematograph 'The Stolen Child' (film representing with great fidelity the stealing of a child by a street beggar, its subsequent restoration to its mother and arrest of the thief!)

An article described how the Commanding Officer, Adj. Murray, made brief and suitable remarks at the end of each subject conveying the moral, instructive or religious lesson to be learned... to a total audience of about 2,500.... who had been kept away from visiting the low Music Halls, theatres and even worse places...hundreds of these young men and women will be won for Christ. The entrance price for the evening service was 2d. One Saturday night Adj. Murray claimed that he had 2,900 people present for a Cinematograph and Lantern service.

'The War Cry' stated that there were over thirty Citadels in Britain showing films at this time. One operator, Capt. Narroway, had travelled around Britain with his Cinematograph and Lantern. At one unnamed Citadel he showed 3,000ft of film to a packed crowd. The films which were shown included William Booth receiving the Foreign Contingents at the International Congress and the Funeral Procession of Emma Booth-Tucker.

Adjutant Murray's success at both Tottenham Citadel and later at Glasgow City Hall where he gave regular Cinematograph services to congregations which had increased from 800 – 3,000 resulted in a large number of conversions. He stated that "I invariably open the Meeting with all the lights up, as if it were an ordinary service. I then have prayer after which the lights are lowered and a well known Salvation song is thrown upon the sheet. This is followed by a Cinematograph Picture. As the latter passes through, I relate the story to which it refers... the lights are then turned up, the announcements for the ensuing week are made, and the collection is taken. While the latter is being completed, either the band plays or the songsters sing."

William Booth's "Orders and Regulations for Field Officers of the Salvation Army" was published for the 1904/05 season. It included a section on Magic Lanterns, however, there was no specific mention of the Cinematograph. Regulation No. 8 stated:- "It must ever be borne in mind that the use of Lanterns or any other special attraction in our Meetings must be kept in harmony with the principles and aim of the Army – the Glory of God in the Salvation of Souls." Another section included a reference to allowing only Salvationists to conduct Lantern Services, and that all Lantern Services must end with "an appeal to the Penitent Form or Consecration Alter". Lantern Services could only be used by the S.A. when the public were invited and all slides had to be approved by S.A. HQ.

For the 1905/6 season Adjutant Murray contributed to an article on the Spiritual and Financial value of the Cinematograph. He stated that any film about which he had the least doubt would be viewed privately first and would be rejected if the film contained anything objectionable. He recommended that films from the Walturdaw Company should be used for the Sunday evening services. These included 'The Life of Christ', 'Joseph and His Brethren', 'The Story of Moses', 'The Good Samaritan', 'The Prodigal Son' and 'The Judgement of Solomon'.

Another section of the same article was written by Major Albert Osborn who had been in charge of Congress Hall. He claimed to have been the first S.A. Officer to include animated pictures between the Lantern slides on a regular basis. He stated that he obtained his animated photos from a large central library (which he didn't name) and that the service usually opened with an illustrated hymn, after which the congregation prayed. This was followed by a short story which was told using about fifteen

THE SALVATION ARMY AND THE CINEMATOGRAPH 1897 - 1929

Stills from Salvation Army films Top: Filmed on an outdoor set showing the General and his daughter, Eva Booth, and Frederick Cox, Row 2: Salvation Army band at a London outdoor meeting and Salvation Army Social workers, Row 3: Motor Crusade in 1904 Bottom Row: Indian delegates leaving the International Congress Hall in the Strand in 1904 and the General taking the salute at the Crystal Palace.

THE SALVATION ARMY AND THE CINEMATOGRAPH 1897 - 1929

*Top 3 rows feature stills from the Salvation Army film of General Booth's visit to the Holy Land with top right Florence Biddington and the last two images showing the Camera used in the filming.
Bottom: The General's visit to the USA with bottom right Frederick Cox and William and Eva Booth.*

Lantern slides. Two animated pictures came next with another short salvation or Gospel story plus several more living pictures. He stated further that the principle they adopted at Congress Hall was to allow the people who attended to have a 'SATURDAY NIGHT SMILE' which meant showing a number of humorous pictures. He stated that the final animated picture usually illustrated the downfall of a thief, or a would-be temperance subject with a sound moral lesson to it. Osborn stated that attendance increased from about 100 to over 2000 in the three years that film had been shown at Congress Hall. During the ten minute interval refreshments could be purchased and any profit made would be divided between the venue and the Juniors. Osborn had bought the projector out of profits made from the use of the Cinematograph on Saturday nights. He claimed that the 26ft. picture size was the largest in London comparing it with the average 18-20ft. Prior to purchasing the projector he had paid a firm between £2.15/- and £4.4/- per night for films and projection equipment. He now only paid out £1.10.6d per week (this was presumably for films). He stated that his weekly admission takings amounted to £12 or £13. This had resulted in the Corps debt of £550 being paid off in full. Each evening service lasted approximately one and three quarter hours. He had originally charged 3d. for admission but later reduced this to 2d. with children at half price. He estimated that on average at least 700 of those who attended were young people aged between 16 - 20 yrs. Major Osborn stated that they deliberately refrained from showing sensational films. For one lecture which he gave entitled 'From the Blind Beggar Public House to the Clapton University' Osborn had included photographic and oral testimony which he had researched himself.

The General en route to the Holy Land

At South Tottenham Citadel, Adj. Ernest Sutton ran the Cinematograph services. Originally he had received some opposition from his colleagues but had persuaded them to give him a one month trial. He used posters and handbills to advertise these Cinematograph services. He hired the equipment from the Walturdaw Company at £2.10/- a night, which included the Cinematograph machine, two gas cylinders and one large spool of film for each show. The 1,600 feet of film to be shown was interspersed with slides, short stories and illustrated songs. He stated that Saturday night attendance rose from about 50 to 500. Adj. Sutton stated that he required at least fifteen assistants for each evening, eight of whom would serve out the refreshments during the interval in the gallery and in the auditorium. He also considered it important to have a rehearsal of the films to be shown on the previous night. An example of one of his Saturday night services is as follows:

1) Opening Song 'War Cry' – Band leading

2) Prayers

3) Selections by Band

4) Lights are lowered and the sheet drops as the programme for the evening is announced

5) Illustrated Song – 'Rock of Ages'

6) Cinematograph: 'Mountaineering in Switzerland' and 'Logging in Canada'

7) Recitation 'The Road to Heaven' illustrated by Limelight views.

8) Cinematograph 'Rescued by Rover'

9) Illustrated Song - 'O God our Help' (sung by the band behind the sheet)

10) Cinematograph: 'Nell and the Burglar'

11) Cinematograph: 'Life of Moses'

12) Doxology (thrown up on the sheet)

13) Reading 'The Life of General Gordon' with Limelight views

Ernest Sutton was the lecturer for the evening, while two of his assistants worked the projector and the slides.

On March 2nd 1905 William Booth had set out with a group of fellow officers on a pilgrimage to the Holy Land after which they would journey to Australia. They took a steamer from Marseilles arriving in Port Said on March 7th. They then took another steamer to

THE SALVATION ARMY AND THE CINEMATOGRAPH 1897 - 1929

Part of the copyright record of photograph taken by Henry Howse on Mt. Calvary - Florence Biddington is on the left-hand side

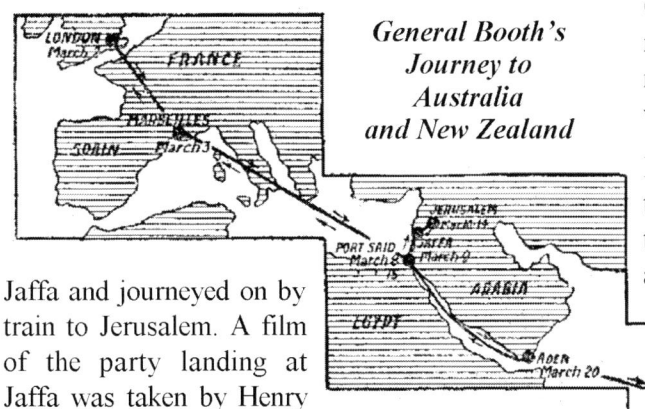

THE SALVATION ARMY AND THE CINEMATOGRAPH 1897 - 1929

General Booth's Journey to Australia and New Zealand

Jaffa and journeyed on by train to Jerusalem. A film of the party landing at Jaffa was taken by Henry Howse. They stayed at the house of Miss Arnott who ran a school for Arab children. William Booth held his first Meeting there at 10am.

At Jerusalem they stayed with a Dutch S.A. Officer, Adj. Nuttall who worked in the slums. She was a wealthy woman in her own right and had rented a house for them to stay in. On the Monday (March 8th) the group visited the Tomb of the Kings, the Garden of Gethsemane, Calvary and the Pool of Bethseda.

On the top of Calvary William Booth signed a manifesto calling upon the Army and the Churches to make a more 'out and out desperate struggle for the world's salvation'.

Frederick Cox stated in his notebook; "At the gate of the Tomb of the Kings they had been met by lepers, their withered faces all wrinkled, with their handless arms held out to them and their imploring voices pleading and with their leprous sores exposed to view. They re-iterated their plaintive wails 'Backsheath, backsheath'." Cox

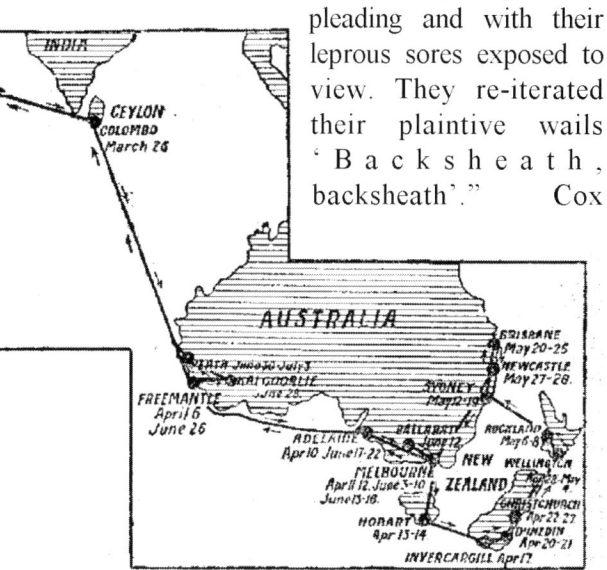

This map shows the route General Booth took on his long Australian Campaign, and the principal cities he visited. The arrows indicate the outward and return journeys.

continued; "It is a lovely day and as we pass up the hill towards the Russian Church, we find at least one thousand Russian pilgrims, poor and ragged and weary, and dirty maybe, but oh, so in earnest."

In a letter, Frederick Cox mentions Florence Biddington, the sister of his wife, Amy, and stated "We are now in Gethsemane – and under the Tree of Agony we all knelt and prayed, the General leading and Florrie standing immediately behind him. The General has been so kind to her – she met us at the station and presented some white violets to him. The General invited her to join his party and today we have been to many places and Florrie is in the Cinematograph pictures. We have been to the Tombs of the Kings, Gethsemane, Olivet, Calvary, Solomon's Quarries and Bethseda and along the Via Dolorosa. – Now I am writing this in the Meeting. Florrie is sitting just in front of me and cheers me with a smile now and then. I have been playing the organ so I am writing unobserved under the cover of the keyboard."

In two letters to her sister, Amy, Florence Biddington, who had been a medical missionary in Palestine for sixteen years recalled the day's events

William Booth on Mt. Calvary (Note film camera on the right)

"WILLIAM BOOTH, GOD'S SOLDIER". Page 12.

OUTSIDE INST. *Workhouse*	Now the General has stopped outside a Poor Law Institution in a wayside village to speak to the people./
End Reel 2.	
SHIP. *Reel 3.* *Holy Land* *Jaffa*	In 1905 the General set out to visit Australia, spending a few days in the Holy Land on the way. Here he is going ashore at Jaffa, where, - his journal records - they were received by the cinematograph./ He is accompanied by his faithfull Aide-de-Camp Lawley./
CAB.	The General's programme was a full one./
MOSQUE. *of Omar* *Solomon's Temple*	He visited the Mosque of Omar, built on the site of Solomon's Temple./
BETHANY. *House of Martha Mary* WAILING WALL. *gave alms to beggar*	At Bethany he visited the house of Martha and Mary. In Jerusalem he visited the Wailing Wall of the Jews, and gave alms to a beggar. He described the Wailing Wall as one of the most pathetic scenes he had ever witnessed./
GARDEN OF GETH.	He entered the Garden of Gethsemane./
	(Music.)
GENERAL PRAYS.	Here he knelt down and prayed./
	(Music.)
PROCLAMATION ON CALVARY	The climax of his visit to the Holy Land was when he visited Mount Calvary and read a Manifesto he had prepared calling on all who name the name of Christ to follow His example and make a desperate effort on behalf of the Salvation of the lost world. This Manifesto was reproduced in the press of countries every-where./
	(Music.)
GENERAL IN LONDON STATION.	The General arriving home after his long tour is met by Bramwell Booth, the Chief-of-Staff, and Commissioner Hay.
FREEDOM OF CITY.	Later that same year a great honour befell him. He received the Freedom of the City of London at a ceremony at the Guildhall.

Film scenario by Bernard Booth

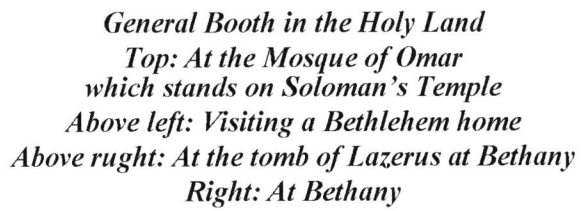

THE SALVATION ARMY AND THE CINEMATOGRAPH 1897 - 1929

General Booth in the Holy Land
Top: At the Mosque of Omar
which stands on Soloman's Temple
Above left: Visiting a Bethlehem home
Above rught: At the tomb of Lazerus at Bethany
Right: At Bethany

Salvation Army postcard reproductions taken from the cinematograph films.

on Calvary. Her letters were forwarded c/o the Rev. H. Sykes, of the Church Missionary Society in Jerusalem. The first letter, dated 19th March 1905 stated; "The Visit to Calvary was intensely exciting, and under great difficulty and danger. But the Army flag floating over the General was photographed and in one I was holding the end of the flag steady. I hope before long to tell you about that achievement, as the authorities have received orders to stop any outdoor Meetings, as I know that soldiers were on watch everywhere."

In a second letter to her sister on March 24th Florence wrote "Do you remember me telling you long ago that the government had built a wall around Calvary? This is since Moody held his meetings there, when the people who assembled trod upon the graves (for I must explain that Calvary has long been a Mohammedan burial ground). This so enraged the people that no-one can hold a meeting there now. Well dear, we arrived at the gate, Howse got one of the men to carry the camera box and went on quickly ahead up the hill.... Fred had hold of the General, Col. Roussel, the flag, and I, the staff. We passed on quickly, leaving Nicol and Lawley to talk and help our guide. The gate-keeper threatened all sorts of things to our guide if he did not insist upon our return; still on we went right to the top. The General was greatly moved as he signed a particular document facing the city. As to sing was impossible, we repeated 'When I survey the Wondrous Cross'. My eyes and ears were fixed upon our hostile surroundings; I 'know' the Muslim mind and what they are capable of doing. As we turned to leave, I began to pick up some wild flowers and gave them to the General. Whereupon some of the children began to gather for us. Our guide gave the gate-keeper a big backsheath and began to talk in Arabic; but until then I kept quiet, only watching, lest they should seize the camera, and I was prepared to interfere as the government people have a trick of opening the camera and destroying the films. The camera was on its stand and the black gate-keeper made straight for that and seized one of its legs, but somehow Howse's quiet, steady eye and our marching up to the camera, arrested the man's attention and at least one stone aimed at us failed to leave the hand."

On March 9th, John Lawley recalled that "the next morning William Booth visited Bethlehem to see where Jesus was born – on the way he passed the tomb where the wife of Jacob was buried. He entered the Church of the Nativity in Bethlehem – he visited the stable in which Christ was said to be born and prayed. He next visited the Temple where Solomon's Temple may have stood." Later William Booth was driven through the real part of Jerusalem as Lawley recalled – "The house of a rich man was pointed out and the spot where Lazarus, full of sores, was licked by dogs – both died. His next call was the Jews Wailing Wall, a place outside the city walls yet right up against the walls – every Friday, men, women and children assemble against the walls and weep bitterly."

Frederick Cox wrote in his notebook, "We have just got back from a visit to Bethlehem. The skies were blue and the 'Shepherds' Fields as green as emeralds. Past long strings of laden camels and flocks of pretty brown and black and white sheep, shepherd led, we rode to the beautiful City of David, the Birthplace of Jesus, and in the Church of the Nativity, knelt and prayed at the Manger... we went with Florrie to a house where we saw 'two women grinding at the mill'. The General turned the handle and so did I."

Florence Biddingtion had also mentioned the trip to Bethlehem in her letter to her sister dated March 19th. She wrote, "the Cinematograph was at work in all these places except perhaps the Holy Sepulchre... the General and Fred had left leaving me with Howse, the photographer and Col. Roussel and Lawley. Howse was anxious to obtain a thoroughly natural group and he had his wish for the people thoroughly entered heart and soul into the fun. Towards the end we stepped into the picture and a more laughable picture I am sure never was taken before in Bethlehem."

On the final day of their visit to the Holy Land (March 10th) William Booth visited the Holy Sepulchre, the Judgement Hall, Bethany (the ruins of the home of Mary and Martha), the Tomb of Lazarus and Absalom's Tomb.

They were due to leave Jaffa on March 12th but their departure had to be delayed for a day due to windy weather. Instead, another meeting was arranged at 8pm at Miss Newton's Mission hall to a group of one hundred and fifty native girls. William Booth had conducted four meetings during his stay in Jerusalem. Lt Col. Roussel and Henry Howse were left behind in Jerusalem to hold further meetings. The following day as Lawley recalled; "twelve native oarsmen rode William Booth to the steamer and that four stalwart natives carried him on board up a ladder." On March 15th 1905, William Booth and the rest of his party left Port Said on SS Victoria bound for Australia (via Colombo).

'The War Cry' of March 25th 1905 contained a reference which stated that Cinematograph views had been taken of the chief events of William Booth's tour in Jerusalem. It stated that a special operator had been sent out by arrangement with the Walturdaw Co. of 3, Dean Street, London, and that this Company worked in conjunction with the S.A Trade HQ. Pictures taken included the Disembarkation at Jaffa, the Reception at Jerusalem, Scenes at Gethsemane, the Demonstration on Mt. Calvary and views descriptive of Eastern life and customs. One of these films had been copyrighted at Stationers Hall in London by the Walturdaw Co. –'William Booth on Mt. Calvary' (his moral encyclical to the world). The films were shown at the Royal Albert Hall on September 9th 1905 with William Booth present – "vivid representations of life in the Holy Land were interlarded with moving pictures of the General's historic visit to Palestine, chief of which were:- His landing at Jaffa, Leaving the Mosque at Omar, The Visit to the Garden of Gethsemane, and The Signing on Mt. Calvary of his Manifesto to the world."

The S.A. Catalogue of October 1906 contained details of the following films (a short compilation of these films are included in 'William Booth, God's Soldier').

List of films in S.A. Catalogue: October 1906

1) The General Landing at Joppa.

2) The General on Calvary.

3) Gethsemane.

4) The Mosque of Omar.

5) The Grave of Lazarus.

6) Boating on the River Jordan.

7) Drawing Water from the Nile.

8) Grinding at the Mill.

Had Henry Howse left the S.A. by this date? There may have been a parting of the ways. In a letter of April 7th 1905 William Booth referred to a letter from Bramwell (Booth) stating; "there are problems with the photographic reproductions which Walturdaw are going to issue as a series of postcards, and there are also problems with Howse and the Cinematograph business". However, William Booth wrote that it was too long a story to go into and did not detail the exact problem. On April 4th 1905 Lt. Col. Roussel journeyed to India for a two month visit. Did Howse go with him? In any event Cinematograph pictures were taken which will be considered in some detail in Part III.

The Salvation Army Penge Band. Henry Howse played one of the two Eb bombardons.

During William Booth's visit to Australia, where he was accompanied by Lawley, Nicol and Frederick Cox, Cinematograph pictures had also been taken, probably by the Biorama Company run by Perry. In September 1905 at the Royal Albert Hall, London, a film of Australian Training Homes was shown – "Cadets who were watching, split the darkness with a terrific cheer"(as reported in "The War Cry").

William Booth spent his 76th birthday at Melbourne before returning to Britain, arriving at Dover on July 31st 1905. The following day he began his second motor tour of Britain, starting at Folkestone and keeping up a hectic schedule until he reached Crystal Palace on September 5th. One of places he visited was Horsham in Sussex, where he stood outside the workhouse gates preaching for their abolition.

Also shown at the Royal Albert Hall on September 9th 1905 was a film of his second motor campaign which was accompanied by the S.A. Staff Band. The final slide of the evening's performance contained William Booth's motto: "Every hour and every power for Christ and duty". A list of some of the places he visited was included in the 1906 S.A. Film Catalogue as follows: (a sequence is included in 'William Booth, God's Soldier').

1) Arrival at Stirling.

2) Entering Forfar.

3) Entering Dundee.

4) Leaving Dundee.

5) A Breakdown on the Way.

6) Arrival at Darlington.

7) Arrival at Blantyre.

8) Arrival at Nuneaton.

9) Arrival at Holbeach.

10) Arrival at Rugby.

Between March and September 1905, George Bernard Shaw had written his play "Major Barbara" which he set in January 1906. The central character was the daughter of an arms manufacturer (not unlike William Booth) who was manufacturing aerial torpedoes for the Russo-Japanese conflict. The firm was called 'Undershaft and Lazarus'. The play was premiered at the Royal Court in November 1905.

A report in "The War Cry" stated that the play was woven more or less around William Booth's slum work and that the second act was set in a S.A. 'doss house' and displayed many of William Booth's views which he had given on his religious campaigns for rescuing the poor.

During 1906, Cinematograph services were held at Norland House by Ensign and Mrs Henderson, as well as at Regent Hall in Oxford Street and Congress Hall at Clapton. At the Congress Hall, where Major Robertson was in charge and which had a capacity of 3000-4000 people, the congregation would stand 3-4 deep around the barriers to the Cinematograph, which was not enclosed in an iron box as the L.C.C. regulations specified. Most of the audience were young.

Comm. Frederick Booth-Tucker, the Foreign Secretary for the S.A. gave two talks at Paddington Green Citadel on "Lights and Shadows of S.A. Warfare in America, India and Japan!" These were illustrated with Limelight and Cinematograph pictures.

1953 cartoon strip - a modern Major Barbara!

THE SALVATION ARMY AND THE CINEMATOGRAPH 1897 - 1929

Crowds of young people have been brought in from the streets by Clapton's Saturday Night Cinematograph Service, which has been an increasing local attraction during the last few months - 'War Cry' 5th May 1906

A Jolly Night for the Youngsters. Section of a gathering of 1,500 children who, in the Congress Hall, Clapton, were given a tea and afterwards entertained with music, song, and a cinematograph display - 'The Social Gazette' 16th January 1909

At Northampton Citadel the Cinematograph season started on Saturday, January 13th 1906. There were three Cinematograph items in the Programme (out of a total of fifteen). Items 4, 6 and 12 were Cinematograph spools lasting between 15-20 minutes each. Attendance for Saturday nights reached about 800 whereas during the weekdays it only reached about 80. The aim was to "keep young people from being drawn into the vortex of folly". Gallery seats cost 3d. while ground floor seats were 2d. Children under 10yrs old got in for half price.

Between July 24th and August 29th 1906, William Booth set out on his third tour of Britain by car and travelled between Inverness and Plymouth, including a visit to Dartmoor Prison.

On 22nd September 1906, at the Royal Albert Hall, a memorial service for the thirty six S.A. Officers "Promoted To Glory" in the past year was held. Their final messages were reproduced by means of the Cinematograph.

During October 1906 the S.A. took a major decision to issue their own Catalogue. In future both Cinematograph machines and films would be available for hire. It seems that the S.A. had arrived at a business accommodation with the Gaumont Company, whose London offices were based at 22, Cecil Court, (off Charing Cross Road). A summary of other S.A. related film productions is included. (See Appendix).

On June 16th 1906 Frederick Booth-Tucker married for the third time. His new wife was Lt. Col. Mary (Minnie) Reid. Together, they gave several Cinematograph services. In October, at Holloway 1 (Citadel) forty two conversions occurred. Also that month at the Queen's Theatre, Leeds, "one hundred and seven souls went to the mercy seat". The following month they both set sail to India. In December 1906, the Walturdaw Co. which had been previously associated with both the S.A. and Henry Howse, issued a series of films on Indian scenes and life which had been filmed by a "Mr Howes". The Company stated that they had sent a developing plant out to him in India. The same month the S.A. published a photo of the Penge Staff Band which included "H. House" with an Eb bombardon. The article stated that he had been a bandsman for seventeen years having been saved twenty one years previously.

The years 1907-1909 saw a marked decline in the use of the Cinematograph in Britain by the S.A. This was probably due mainly to the Cinematograph fire at Newmarket Town Hall on September 7th 1907, which resulted in three women losing their lives. The Cinematograph machine had not been enclosed in an iron box and the premises also did not have a music licence. The S.A. does not seem to have adhered to those requirements for most of their own Cinematograph 'services'.

The Newmarket deaths were followed in January 1908 by yet another tragedy in which sixteen children were crushed to death during a panic which took place at a Cinematograph show in Barnsley. These two tragic events would have affected S.A. thinking and behaviour as had the Cinematograph fire in Paris in May 1897. In January 1909 there was a reference in 'The Social Gazette' to a recent Cinematograph fire that had occurred in the East End of London. The article also mentioned the "dreadful

51

THE SALVATION ARMY AND THE CINEMATOGRAPH 1897 - 1929

CHILDREN'S FATAL PANIC AT A SOUTHSEA PICTURE ENTERTAINMENT.

Rose Kirkby, aged 14, who was bruised and very severely shaken.

Lilian Nightingale, one of the two children detained in hospital last night.

Harry Graham, aged 12, who was killed in the panic. Through a cruel hoax, his parents did not hear of his death for several hours.

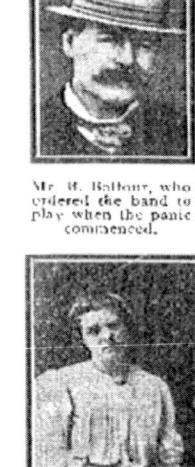

Mr. B. Balfour, who ordered the band to play when the panic commenced.

Arthur Berry, who was separated from Graham during the crush.

Phyllis Harvey, aged three and a half years, who was badly crushed, and is suffering severely from shock.

Mr. and Mrs. Graham, parents of Graham, the dead boy, with all their children.

James Duffin, aged 12, who was also badly crushed.

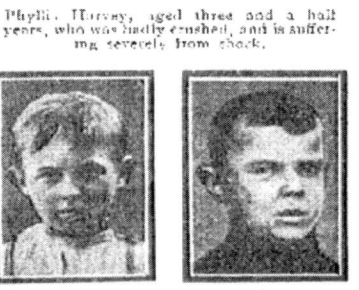

Arthur Ward, aged 7, whose face was badly bruised.

(A) Door in which the children were jammed in escaping from the gallery. (B) Staircase where the crush was most severe.

Emmie Lewis, aged 8 years, who was severely bruised.

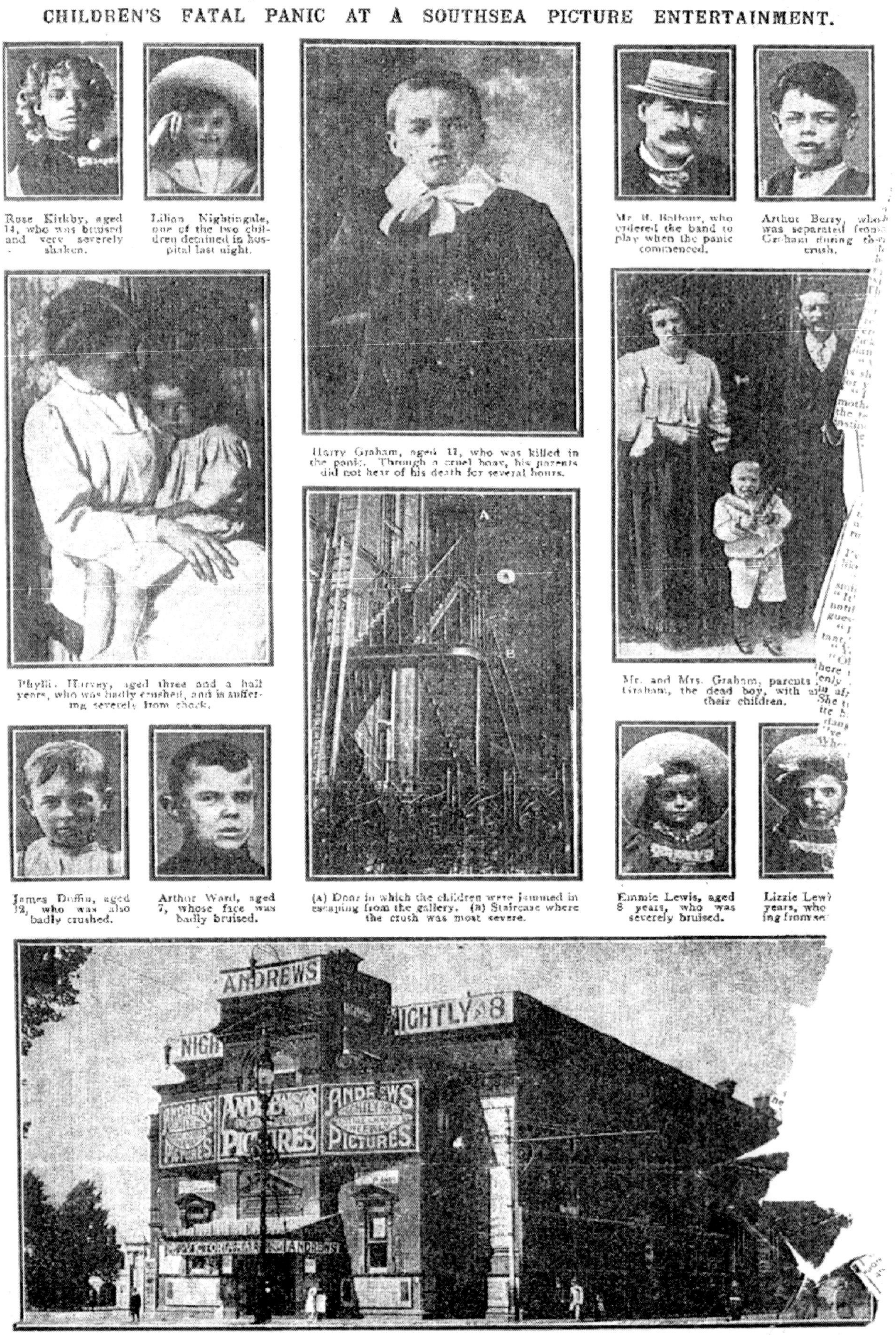

Lizzie Lewis, years, who...

Extract from the 'Daily Mirror' of 16th August 1909 concerning the false alarm of fire at the Victoria Hall in Southsea which resulted in the death of Harry Graham and the injury of eight other children.

THE SALVATION ARMY AND THE CINEMATOGRAPH 1897 - 1929

GREAT MUSICAL FESTIVAL AT THE ROYAL ALBERT HALL.

THE
WAR CRY

OFFICIAL GAZETTE OF THE SALVATION ARMY.

No. 1,633.]   LONDON, SATURDAY, NOVEMBER 9, 1907.   [PRICE ONE PENNY.

President Roosevelt.   The General.

THE GENERAL MEETS PRESIDENT ROOSEVELT IN WASHINGTON.

The "White House" in the background is the official residence of the American President, and it was here where The General lunched.

53

National Headquarters
120, West 14th Street.
New York.

2.

Eva reports to me that Parker took some wonderful moving pictures of me at Boston: that the first Boston theatre bought the copyright of them so far as this country goes, and that the theatre manager says that the audience rises with distraction at the point where I take off my hat to the crowd. He wrote and informed the International Trade Headquarters about these pictures, to which they replied that they had no use for this sort of thing, or something to that effect. Will you kindly get me an explanation of this.

There is nothing more that I need say just now.

Believe me,

Yours affectionately,

William Booth

General.

An extract from a letter by William Booth to Bramwell Booth, October 1907, St. Louis

catastrophe at Barnsley" and considered that more careful supervision was required. The article went on to criticise other dangers that were associated with "these vulgar exhibitions and side-shows which were thickly planted in the poorest and most densely populated localities - too often the entertainment is a tawdry garish affair which is positively harmful to young people – according to the present state of the law any cheap-jack can hire a Hall and Cinematograph and proceed to extract the pennies and half-pennies off young children without the slightest regard for the unhealthy atmosphere, and illicit excitement upon which many such enterprises mainly thrive."

From this it seems evident that by the end of 1908, the S.A. was pulling back from its involvement in the use of the Cinematograph both for moral and practical reasons. The 1908 Children's Act was followed by the 1909 Cinematograph Act which insisted on strict regulations when the Cinematograph was in use and when children were in the audience. Even so, when the L.C.C. made their check of the S.A. premises at the Rink in Oxford Street, they found that the venue had not yet applied for a licence to show films. They were still regularly showing films on Saturdays in the winter season. G. Manning later recalled; "It was during Major Robertson's second stay that the Corps ran a series of 'Saturday Night Pops' for the children – usually we had about 1,500 who paid 1d. for admission – on one occasion a fire broke out in the upper rooms of No. 271 Oxford Street (which overlooked the 'Rink') There was a panic, no one was hurt."

When William Booth made his second journey to the USA and Canada towards the end of 1907 a record of part of his trip was filmed by Edward Justus Parker who, four years earlier, had filmed Emma's funeral. In a letter which William Booth wrote to his son Bramwell in London he stated that "Eva reports to me that Parker took some wonderful moving pictures of me at Boston; that the First Boston Theatre bought the copyright of them so far as this country goes, and that the theatre manager says that the audience rises with distraction at the point where I take my hat off to the crowd; he wrote and informed the International Trade HQ about these pictures to which they replied that they had no use for this sort of thing, or something to that effect. Will you kindly get me an explanation of this?" Four short films from this visit survive at the BFI.

During 1908, Charles Ollis seems to have taken over the running of the Cinematograph and Lantern Department at S.A. HQ following Howse's departure. As part of the series of Animated Pictures shown at Regent Hall (the Rink) on Wednesday June 17th he included one for a young people's demonstration. In August he was in Charge of the Tableaux Vivant services. The 'Living Pictures' which were shown were all scriptural subjects. He took them on tour to a number of Citadels in the London area, charging 1d. as the entrance fee. In November 1908 he was preparing Shadowgraph stories for the upcoming Christmas season.

One edition of "The War Cry" from January 1909 contains a photograph of children attending a Cinematograph performance at Congress Hall, Clapton. It stated that 1,500 children were present. In March 1909 as the S.A. Journal stated; "it is painful to think that for a penny, a young boy may have his moral nature poisoned for life regarding 'Funland, Fairyland and Wonderland!'" That month, 'The Field Officer' commented on the 1908 Children's Act, suggesting that if the Cinematograph is shown in a building with a gallery, sufficient staff attendants would be required to monitor their safety.

"The War Cry" reported, in August 1909, that at an open-air meeting at Southsea II on a Sunday afternoon, the mother of an 11year old boy, who had been killed the previous afternoon, asked for a special prayer to be said on his behalf. The article stated that a stampede had occurred at a Cinematograph entertainment after the cry of 'Fire' had been falsely raised. There was a mad rush in which eight other children were injured. The 'Daily Mirror' of 16th August 1909 reported on the fatality at The Victoria Hall in Southsea and included a photograph of Harry Graham, who had died in the panic which had occurred during a matinee performance by 'Andrew's Pictures'.

Several adverts also appeared in the S.A. Trade Press from individuals wishing to sell their Cinematograph equipment. One un-named officer from Folkestone advertised a combined Cinematograph and Lantern for sale at £4.15/- when it had originally been purchased for 15 guineas. Henry Nottridge from Boston, Lincs, wanted £20 for his Gaumont Cinematograph and accessories. He stated that it had originally cost £45.3.4d and had only been used twelve times. By contrast Adj. and Mrs. Ward from Tunbridge Wells had purchased a Cinematograph in 1909. They found that their audiences swelled to between 400 and 500 a week. These were mainly young people who came to see the S.A. pictures and to learn the S.A. choruses.

THE SALVATION ARMY AND THE CINEMATOGRAPH 1897 - 1929

Shadow Scene on the platform, with Carol Singers at the side

SHADOW II.—Drunkard's Home-coming

SHADOW III.—Saved Father's Return

SHADOW IV.—Prayer

SHADOW VI.—Sick Child

SHADOW VIII.—Happy Old Age

A selection of Shadowgraph scenes prepared by Charles Ollis in November 1908

THE SALVATION ARMY AND THE CINEMATOGRAPH 1897 - 1929

Further afield, fresh developments in the use of the Cinematographs as a proselytising tool were taking place. For the winter campaign of 1908/9, Mrs. Col. Povlsen had arranged with International HQ to allow her to show Cinematograph films in Denmark.

Several of William Booth's family were still showing Cinematograph Pictures – his youngest son, Herbert, who, having resigned from the S.A. in 1902 had settled in the USA and during 1909 was on a world tour with his Cinematograph lecture depicting The Life of The Early Christians. In November 1909 he gave one of these lectures in Glasgow. 'The Bioscope' stated; "Herbert Booth had organised a company of living models numbering 600 – men, women and children to act the several parts. He had scenery painted – an open-air stage created – models posed – a picture taken for every forty words spoken – when the camera was illustrated by still pictures he got the models to act for the Bioscope". Meanwhile Frederick Booth-Tucker had now become the Resident Secretary in India and Ceylon and was intending to use the Cinematograph as an important proselytising tool and would continue to do so throughout his tenure there.

Left: Mrs. Colonel Povlsen, Norway, who saw service in Denmark, Russia, Sweden and Great Britain.

The Salvation Army presents a lantern show during Utrecht's (Holland) historic Fair week

Commissioner Booth-Tucker (Fakir Singh)

PART III
THROUGH INDIA'S CORAL STRAND

The Salvation Army's first known use of the Cinematograph in India was in 1905. It documented part of the farewell tour of the retiring Indian Commissioner Edward Higgins. It also recorded the inspection by the Under Foreign Secretary Lt. Col. Roussel who visited a number of institutions that the S.A. had set up following the famine period that had hit the Indian sub-continent in the 1890's. In 1902, during another famine period Major Jang Bahadur had visited one hundred villages with a Magic Lantern showing 'The Life of Christ'.

On a later trip that Brg. Jang Bahadur (Hunter) made with Major Dayasagar in 1909, they recalled that "They visited the villages by bullock cart which contained their bedding, a Lantern outfit, a medical chest and the 'inevitable gramophone'. A sheet was put up on a long bamboo pole after which they chose to play some suitable selection on the gramophone". Brg. Bahadur also recalled that on the first occasion that he had taken a Magic Lantern to a settlement to show 'The Life of Christ', the women became frightened believing that they could be transported to England.

Comm. Higgins had been ill. He had to have one of his eyes removed, which precipitated his retirement. He had been in India for six years and before leaving to return to London, decided to visit all the major S.A. institutions to give his farewells. After a Conference at Poona for the various Indian territorial commanders, he departed Colombo for London on April 22nd 1905. Roussel had arrived on April 4th and for the next ten days accompanied Higgins on his farewell tour. He joined Higgins at Gujarat along with Brig. Yesu Das, Major Ward and Ensign Gore. One of them reported in 'India's War Cry' that "We paraded before the Cinematograph manipulated by Roussel prior to our last handshake with Higgins."

Mrs. Ensign Strandlund giving an open-air gramophone recital to the leper patients of the Soerabaja colony in Java in 1919

Another report in 'India's War Cry' stated that "The Commissioner (Higgins) accompanied by Lt.Col. Roussel left Bombay by the night mail on Friday April 9th and arrived at Ahmedabad at 7 o'clock the following morning.... As soon as breakfast was over the whole party proceeded to our Girls Industrial School and there they found the girls lined in front of the school ready to 'top chalao' (ie. fire a volley) as the Commissioner and the Colonel passed through the ranks .... At the close of the Colonel's address, the girls went through some drill and physical exercises in a way that reflected credit on Capt. Karmala Bai and her assistants. Before leaving the school the Col. took some Cinematograph pictures of the girls at drill. On Saturday afternoon, the Commissioner, Colonel and Brigadier left Ahmedabad for the Muktipur farm colony at which place they stayed until Monday when they left for Anand."

THE MAGIC LANTERN IN GUJERAT — JESUS

59

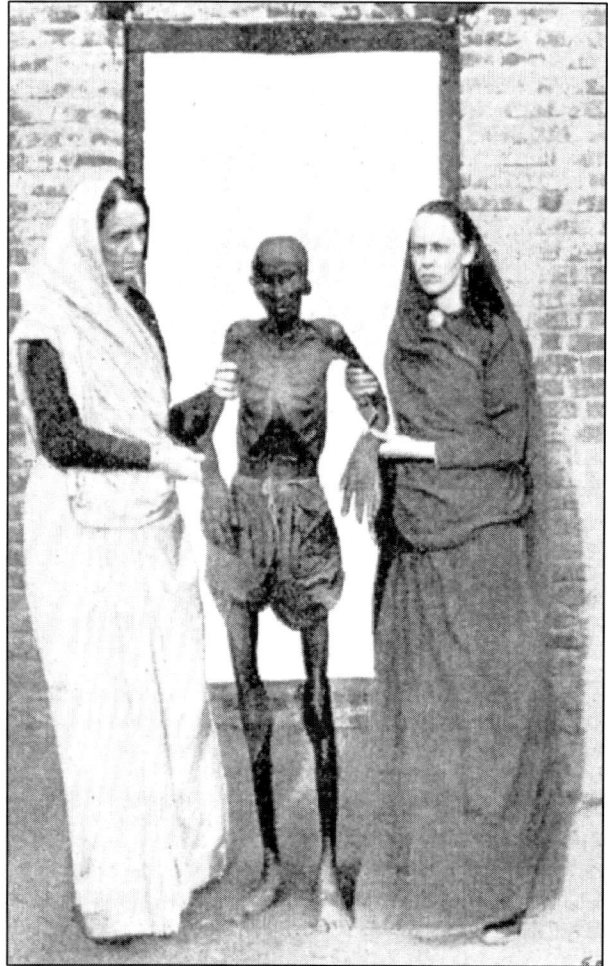

Salvationists working in India. The top picture shows the distribution of food by the Salvation Army as part of their famine relief activities published in 'The War Cry' on 24th October 1908

THE SALVATION ARMY AND THE CINEMATOGRAPH 1897 - 1929

THE WAR CRY, January 18, 1908.

READ OUR ASSURANCE OFFER ON PAGE 16.

THE WAR CRY

OFFICIAL GAZETTE OF THE SALVATION ARMY.

INTERNATIONAL HEADQUARTERS, [Registered at the General Post Office as a Newspaper.] QUEEN VICTORIA STREET

No. 1,643.]   LONDON, SATURDAY, JANUARY 18, 1908.   [PRICE ONE PENNY.

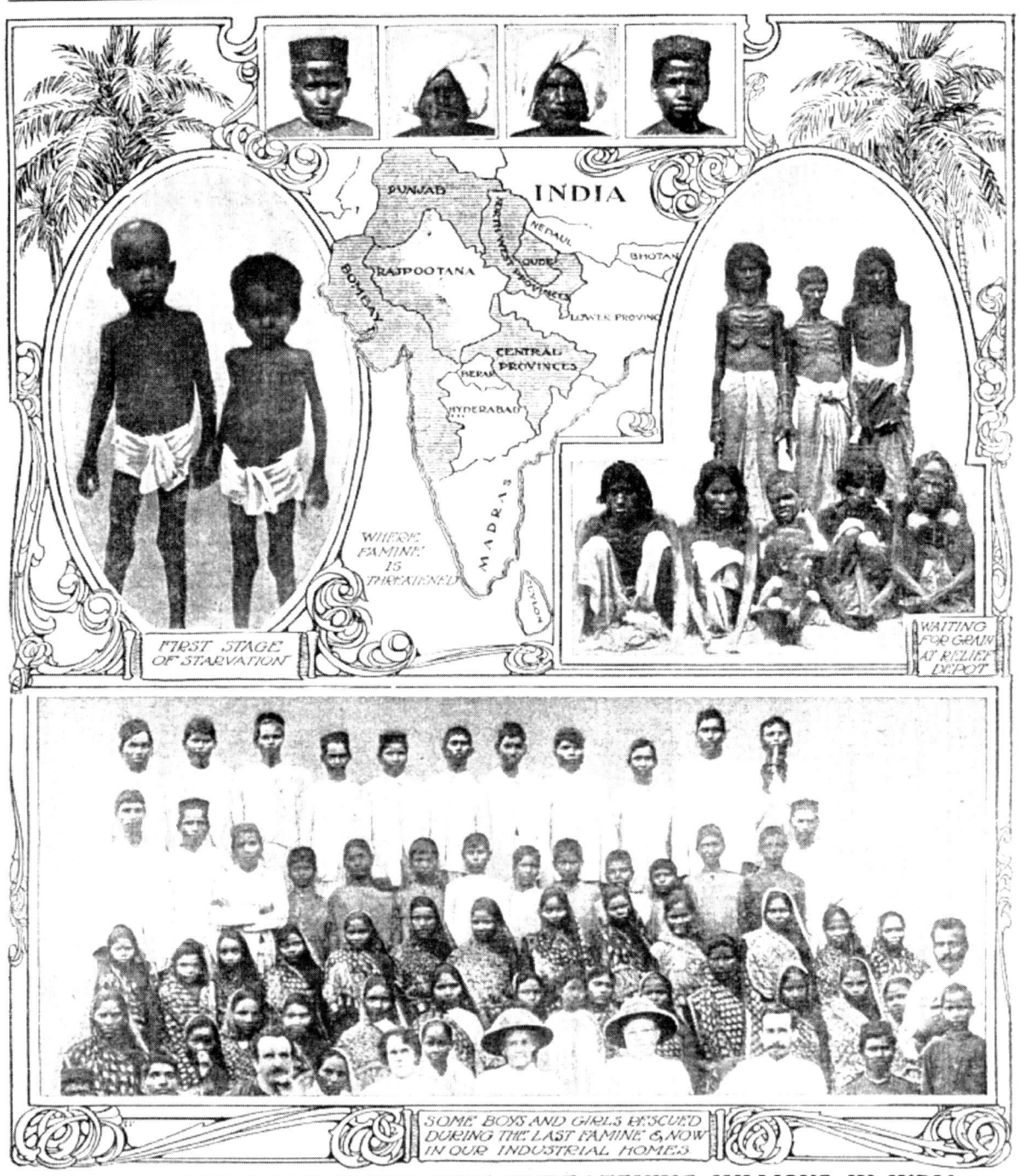

WHERE FAMINE IS THREATENED

FIRST STAGE OF STARVATION

WAITING FOR GRAIN AT RELIEF DEPOT

SOME BOYS AND GIRLS RESCUED DURING THE LAST FAMINE & NOW IN OUR INDUSTRIAL HOMES

FAMINE—THE DARK CLOUD NOW THREATENING MILLIONS IN INDIA.

61

THE SALVATION ARMY AND THE CINEMATOGRAPH 1897 - 1929

The Salvation Army at work in India. Top left: Worshipping a snake goddess in Southern India. Top right: Hindu village temple being demolished after the whole village converted to Christianity after 18 years work there by the Salvation Army. Bottom left: Surrendering an idol to the Salvation Army in Southern India. Bottom right: The god 'Essaki Mardan' and the goddess 'Essaki' removed from the Hindu temple at Kuttukal, Southern India, and handed over to the Salvation Army. The temple is shown being partially demolished, and will be reconstructed for Army purposes.

THE SALVATION ARMY AND THE CINEMATOGRAPH 1897 - 1929

Col. Sukh Singh (Blowers) and party entering a village to conduct a meeting

A flag drill

Another article mentioned their visit to the boys at Muktipur - "In the meantime, Lt. Col. Roussel who accompanied the Commissioner and whom we were all delighted to see, was generally surveying the village and schools, with a view to finding a suitable site for taking a picture of the colonists with their wives. The school and industrial boys (the latter carrying their tools), bullocks and carts with all the cattle bringing up the rear, made one long procession for the Cinematograph, and if I am any judge at all, I should say one of the most interesting pictures that, (h)as yet been taken, was the result. He also took another of the boys at drill."

One way in which the villagers were converted was by destroying both the images of their gods as well as the temples they were housed in. An example of this is given in 'The War Cry' in October 1905. It took place at the village of Kalvalie in Southern India. After Ensign Heden had converted the devil-dancers, the S.A. were requested by the villagers to demolish the 'heathen idols' and Hindu temple and to erect a S.A. hall and school in their place:- "In the entrance chamber there was the usual idol, while in the inner shrine the temple implements and a stone god were found. In the temple compound there was the image of a goddess, a huge brickwork god known as 'Sudala Mardan' besides smaller deities... several women Officers took the first steps towards reducing to atoms Pathra Kali, the goddess who is supposed to have the special virtue of preserving life during cholera epidemics."

Teaching the Story of Jesus and His love by the aid of lantern slides in the remote villages of Mid-Java

The group of films taken by Roussel are included in the 1906 S.A. Catalogue, as follows:

1) Girl's Industrial School and Drill at Ahmedabad
2) Procession of Officers, Gomri
3) Muktipur Farm Colony
4) Emery Hospital and Medical Staff
5) Farewell of Commissioner Higgins
6) Boys Industrial School
7) Bullocks drawing Water
8) Anand Hospital – procession of Patients
9) Troupe of Monkeys
10) Tile-making for the Hospital
11) Procession of Guzerati officers
12) Destruction of the God Baptala
13) Village Meeting and Reception

The Prince and Princess of Wales visited India at the end of 1905 at which time the S.A. decided to send reinforcements to help with the proselytising of some of the 300,000,000 inhabitants.

Between December 10th 1906 and February 9th 1907 Frederick Booth-Tucker and Minnie Reid (his wife) made a tour of India as part of his work as the S.A. Foreign Secretary. They adopted the Indian names of 'Fakir Singh' and 'Dutini' respectively and were referred to by these names while they remained in India. They were accompanied by staff Capt. Glanville, his private secretary, who operated the Cinematograph during the lectures given on 'The Life of Christ' and 'The Social Work of the Salvation Army throughout the World'. Glanville also filmed scenes of local interest. Many of the lectures took place in public halls, however, a number were held at dusk in 'Maidan's' in the open air. At Nagercoil, 6,000 people were present and at Ahmedabad a further 10,000. At the Muktipur farm colony twenty two souls sought salvation.

Glanville is spelt in a number of different ways. In an article in "India's Cry" in February 1907 it is spelt Glenville. However, the photographer and film maker who was Comm. Booth-Tucker's secretary was Edwin Glanville, who together with his wife,

Fakir Singh and Dutini being greeted by Travancore Salvationists in South India on their return from the 1914 Congress

THE SALVATION ARMY AND THE CINEMATOGRAPH 1897 - 1929

*The front cover of 'War Cry' on 21st October 1905
showing the destruction of an Indian heathen temple and a goddess*

Photograph showing Salvation Army staff and their children at Simla, including the children of Booth-Tucker and Glanville.

BACK Row (*Elevated*): Harding Robertson, Lincoln Booth-Tucker, Charles Sowton, Brother Falcon.
SECOND Row (*Standing*): Myron Booth-Tucker, Mrs. Adjt. Bedford and wee Frank Bedford, Sergt. Leslie Hipsey, C.-C.G. May Spooner, C.-C.G. Mrs. Lieut.-Colonel Spooner, C.-C.G. Mrs. Brigadier Robertson, C.-C.G. Mrs. Brigadier Hielm, Shoroj Misra, Mrs. Staff-Capt. Richardson, Staff-Capt. Richardson (Corps Officers).
THIRD Row (*Sitting*): Foster Robertson, Adjt. Wm. Bedford (J.S.M.), Bernice Glanville, Susie Robertson, Mina Booth-Tucker, Gertrude Spooner, and Willie Hielm.
FRONT Row (*Sitting*): George Sowton, Reggie Andrews, Jack Young, Grace Robertson, Eva Glanville, John Hipsey, Ian Robertson, and Muriel Booth-Tucker.

Capt. E J Peake was stationed in India until the early 1920's. By 1925 they had returned to Australia. It seems that Glanville had originally worked with Herbert Booth there. In a letter dated 2nd December 1993 to Major Jenty Fairbank, the archivist/director of the S.A. International Heritage Centre, Col. Paul Du Plessis, (Territorial commander of the S.A. T.HQ. in Central India) had forwarded tinted photographs of prints from Lantern slides discovered in his office in 1990. These were later shown to Col. Muriel Booth-Tucker to identify. A letter from Jenty Fairbank of 13th January 1994 stated:- "She was about ten years old at the time and they were on their way from Simla to a house in the hills sixty miles away which they had bought from an American lady. The oranges grown on the estate were sold in aid of army funds. The house was used for holidays. They travelled first by rickshaw and then on foot and they met the Sadhu on the road (this is one of the lantern slide photographs shown to Muriel Booth-Tucker). The picture was taken by the Commissioner's secretary, Brig. Grenville/Glenville (?) who always carried photographic equipment with him. If Muriel was ten at the time this would date the pictures to about 1914".

Booth-Tucker later recalled; "We sped through villages where the plague had been raging.... 'The Life of Christ' as represented by Living Pictures had a marvellous effect. In the words of Hindus who saw them, they had 'read and heard about Christ, but never realised before how much he suffered'. A young caste man exclaimed 'This is enough to break the stoniest heart.'"

On their return to Britain, Booth-Tucker persuaded Minnie Reid as well as Bramwell Booth of his desire to return to India full time. He asked to relocate the S.A. HQ from Calcutta to Simla where the weather

THE SALVATION ARMY AND THE CINEMATOGRAPH 1897 - 1929

Indian Musicians with Dutini

Photographs taken by Glanville including six girls from the Dom criminal tribe

THE SALVATION ARMY AND THE CINEMATOGRAPH 1897 - 1929

Advertisement for Triumph Tea from the 'War Cry' 12 December 1908

would be more conducive to Europeans and where his six children would receive their schooling. On September 11th 1907 Frederick Booth-Tucker was appointed as a special commissioner to the S.A. forces in India and Ceylon. They arrived on September 23rd and began with a Cinematograph lecture at the Town Hall in Emery. They wore native clothes of khaki and red.

Booth-Tucker's arrival in India coincided with the return of a period of famine which was described in some detail in the pages of "The War Cry". In January 1908 Fakir Singh wrote:- "The prospects seem truly appalling. After a good beginning, there has been a sudden and total failure of the monsoon in the Punjab, United Provinces, Central India, and to a less degree in Guzerat and the Marathri country. Food is already at famine prices. Shipments of grain from Karchi have been practically stopped. Not only is the autumn crop in vast tracts a total failure, but the spring sowings have been prevented through the hardness of the ground."

In February 1908, following Bramwell Booth's decision to open an Indian Distress Fund, Fakir Singh stated:- "There is plenty of grain, thanks to the railway, but the people have no money to buy with, and their own stores and savings are exhausted."

In June 1908, "The War Cry" received a letter form Lt. Col. Tej Singh (Fredericks) in which he wrote about the situation in the Punjab as follows:- "The Plague, which has not been so bad during the winter, began to increase in severity in March, and the deaths for April in the Punjab, rose to between 3,500 and 4,000 each week. The intense heat has however checked its progress, and a slight decrease is noticeable. Cholera is again making its appearance, and in the city of Lahore, eighteen deaths have occurred within a week."

One of the ways that the S.A. raised funds to help combat the famine was in marketing their own brand of 'Triumph Tea'. Fakir Singh also decided to introduce the Cassava plant into drought stricken areas in order to prevent future famines from being so serious. Among the S.A. Officers who succumbed in the cholera epidemic was Capt. Harry Howard, the son of Comm. Howard, the S.A.'s Foreign Secretary.

During 1908, the projectionist for their film lectures was Capt. Dayasagar. Early in 1909 Major Ishwar Das (Glanville) returned with his family. He became their chief projectionist as well as having the task of taking films showing the work of the S.A. in India. To give a flavour of how these film lectures were described in "India's War Cry", I have selected seven examples from their first tour of duty between 1907 and 1910 as follows:-

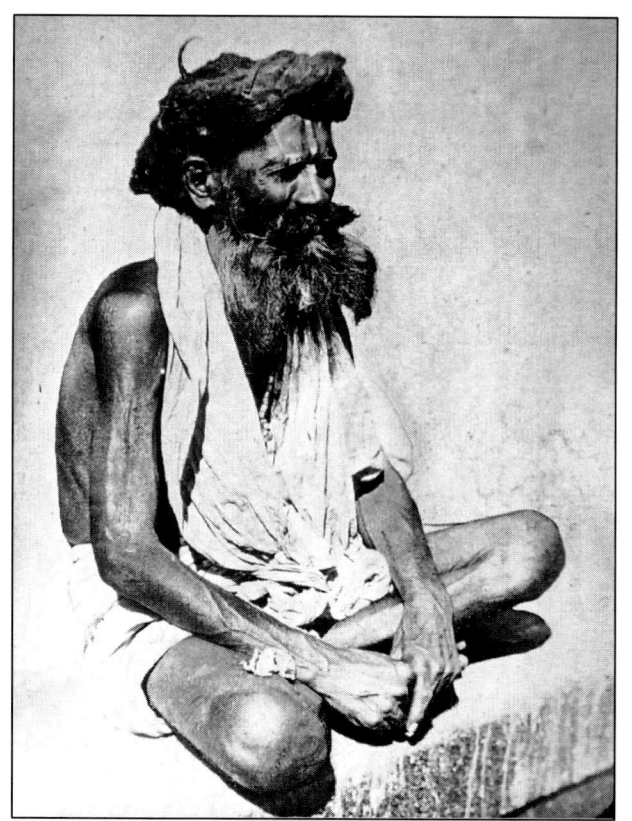

'A Sadhu'?

THE SALVATION ARMY AND THE CINEMATOGRAPH 1897 - 1929

1909

(1) One student commented on a visit to the Victoria Hall, Madras - "I came eight miles to be here tonight. I attend all the Cinematograph shows I can find but had never before been able to find one representing The Life of Christ."

(2) At the Campier Hall, Gorakhpur, a Cinematograph lecture was given on 'The Work of the Salvation Army in Many Lands' - "The scenes of the young man killing his wife when in drink, and of him being led by an army officer to accept Christ in jail, before his execution, appealed to all present."

(3) In Poona, a huge Pandal had been set up to show the Cinematograph lecture on 'The Life of Christ' - "The Cinematograph gave representations of his sufferings and death - one old woman thumped several boys who had accepted an invitation to come to the Saviour."

1910

(4) At Tiruvalla, a Cinematograph picture of a procession was filmed during the opening and dedication of a new divisional HQ. One of the meetings was held in the open air in the campus of The American Missionary Seminary:- "7,000 were seated on the ground, amphitheatre fashion in the soft moonlight, their white wraps and headgear and posture suggesting a huge sheepfold - listen to the laughter and chatter as the amusing and instructing pictures are shown and described by Comm. Fakir Singh. Note the silence of that vast crowd when the earnest appealing pictures of the deathbed of saint and sinner are presented, every word distinctly heard at the very edge of the vast concourse of people."

(5) At Travancore, a large Pandal had been erected for an evening meeting of 5,000. - "Fakir Singh took us to England, the busy thoroughfares and familiar scenes were really a treat - we came back to India - important and interesting natural scenes and many scenes of Army buildings and groups of officers."

(6) Another evening for 3,000 was held at Baptala - "At last we were all seated and settled and we announced the arrival of our specials. Volleys rent the air, the Band boys beat their drums and blew their fifes."

A group from one of the 'criminal tribes'

A group of Bhil women during the famine

69

THE SALVATION ARMY AND THE CINEMATOGRAPH 1897 - 1929

(7) At their HQ at Simla, a Cinematograph meeting was held on a Saturday evening during which - "A number of extra new films descriptive of the S.A. work in India and Ceylon were displayed to a crowded house." On the following evening a new reproduction of 'The Betrayal of Christ' was shown. This was followed by a Cinematograph lecture from Fakir Singh and Dutini entitled 'Among the Doms at Gorukphur' which dealt with the 'Dommara Criminal Tribe'. They stated that the Government in India had been assisted over the past eighteen months by Brig. Hunter of the S.A. with their work with the 'Doms'.

Fakir Singh stated; "Our aim was not only to help the criminal classes, but to get them saved and made into good citizens here and fit for Heaven hereafter."

Fakir Singh stated that the Gorakhpur Dom settlement had been the key to three other similar institutions. He considered the Cinematograph as 'the starter'. Earlier that Sunday morning Fakir Singh had met sixty prisoners in Gorakhpur Jail. During the showing of 'The Life of Christ' those present included 'settlers' who sang with their tom-toms and other musical instruments:- "Our heads were garlanded and after many volleys the meeting started in real Army style". It was at these meetings, held after the Cinematograph lectures, that the S.A. hoped to win over their converts.

What did Fakir Singh mean by 'Criminal tribes'? During the twelve years he was in charge he dedicated his energies to working with these peoples which he wrote about in many articles in a manner which today may appear politically incorrect. However, to give a flavour of his opinions/attitude I will include an extract from one of the interviews he gave on this subject to RDS McMillan published in 'The Wide World Magazine' and later reprinted in 'All the World' in January 1927:- "The 'Crims' as they are called, consist of different sects or castes, who form themselves into tribes, villages, or clans, each sect persuing its own type of crime. There is a sect, for instance, which is addicted solely to house-breaking; another whose members are coiners; .... the members of one tribe devote their time exclusively to jewel robberies in railway trains.... Government keeps a register of them, and whenever a child is born to a 'Crim' family it is automatically placed on the register.... The happy hunting-grounds of the tribes may be said to be Rajputna and Central India, though they are numerous in the United Provinces, Bengal and Madras, while the Punjab has at least 130,000....the railway jewel-thieves are perhaps the most stealthy in their methods. They travel in the trains, and while the women sleep, steal their gems. Indian women wear ear and nose jewels, putting the whole of their savings into these costly ornamentations, which often cost them their lives. The jewel-thief's 'outfit' consists of a tiny knife-blade lashed to the fore-finger. The blade is so razor-keen that the thief is able to slit the lobe of the ear, or the septum of the nose, and remove the gems before the unfortunate sleeper is aware of what is happening.... The Haburahs (another tribe) are not looked upon as dangerous...they had been located near a small town called Kanth, about twenty miles form Moradabad, and the Government wished the S.A. to form a settlement for them outside Moradabad on land provided by the Government.... We were later invited to visit Gorakhpur where the Government proposed to make over to the S.A. some three hundred members of another tribe called the Doms,... the people were confined at night in what were known as 'Dom Khanas', a kind of walled enclosure, where men, women and children were locked in. During the day, they were allowed to go into the city, where many of them were employed as street scavengers and road sweepers. They also begged food from the people for whom they did odd jobs.... A large proportion of the children are either orphans or have parents who are serving long sentences in jail.... The plight of these children is often very sad. When a father is sent to prison the mother secures protection and support by marrying another tribesman, who may himself be imprisoned soon afterwards, when

A Bhil man and his wife

THE SALVATION ARMY AND THE CINEMATOGRAPH 1897 - 1929

THE WAR CRY, May 18, 1907.

CONTINUATION OF THE GENERAL'S VICTORIOUS CAMPAIGN IN JAPAN. (See page 9)

THE WAR CRY

AND

OFFICIAL GAZETTE OF THE SALVATION ARMY.

INTERNATIONAL HEADQUARTERS. [Registered at the General Post Office as a Newspaper] QUEEN VICTORIA STREET

No. 1,608.] LONDON, SATURDAY, MAY 18, 1907. [PRICE ONE PENNY.

MADRAS COLLECTORS' BANDY

DRAWING WATER FOR IRRIGATION PURPOSES

READY FOR AN OPEN-AIR MEETING—TELEGU COUNTRY

MADRAS FISHERFOLK

Pictorial Presentation of Our Work in India—The Army's Greatest Missionary Field.

71

the procedure is repeated by the wife. It is often difficult to discover which among the men who happen to pose as a woman's husband is the actual father of her child."

On April 11th 1910 Fakir Singh, Dutini and Major Ishwar Das returned to England for a war council in order to promote their work with the criminal tribes. They were away for five months. During their absence at least four Cinematograph lectures were given by Major Ranjit Singh and Adj. Amrita Bai. In addition, a particularly dangerous Cinematograph performance was given by Lt. Col. Fredericks to the Pathians at Para Chinar on the N.W. Frontier for the visit of the Viceroy Lord Minto. In an article in 'The War Cry' in June 1910 Lt. Col. Fredericks stated "Para Chinar is situated at the top of the Karram Valley, and is surrounded by unfriendly tribes, who are constantly raiding the districts beyond the snow-capped mountains in Afghanistan. Every man goes about armed to the teeth for it is not safe to travel otherwise. During the long railway journey we passed the famous Dargas Heights, which, in 1896, a British force only captured with great difficulty after thirteen days fighting. From Kirhat, all the railway stations are forts, consisting of four walls, with a loop-hole as a ticket window, two squatting towers, and an iron gateway, which when shut encloses all within....

...The men are tall, fierce and warlike. I had to drive by native vehicle from Thall – where a big military camp was formed – to Para Chinar, taking two days to make the journey. Owing to the impending visit of the Viceroy, soldiers were stationed at every fort, from which, at night, signal lamps continuously flashed, and every prominence was picketed. Native cavalry were sent as a bodyguard for the Viceroy, and even the bearers, cooks, and other servants, while waiting at table, wore revolver and cartridge belts. On three nights I gave Cinematograph exhibitions to the Pathans, who had never seen anything like it before. To look upon these fine fellows makes one covet them for the S.A. ....The Cinematograph, we may say, is widely used in India by the Army for the purpose of making Salvation clear to the native mind."

On his arrival in London, Fakir Singh (Booth-Tucker) gave an interview to "The War Cry" in which he stated that between December 1907 and December 1909, the S.A. had acquired 104 village halls and that there were now 430 schools educating 9,000 children. The 'cream' of these children were sent to one of the S.A. Industrial Schools in order to be trained as possible future S.A. officers. He also confirmed that the S.A. in India had recently demolished in one village two heathen temples, five altars and three idols. They had brought one of the life-size idols with them which they displayed at the Services which they were holding during their stay. Each village housed about 30 families (approx. 150 people). Booth-Tucker made a point of condemning the caste system calling it 'hereditary Trade Unionism with certain religious ceremonies thrown in.' At present he stated that the S.A. cared for 1,000 criminals (out of a total population of 1,000,000 criminals). While in Britain, Booth-Tucker obtained William Booth's agreement on 'reforming the robber tribes of India'.

During their stay in London Fakir Singh and Dutini gave five Cinematograph lectures on 'Indian Life Pictures' including one on June 29th at 8pm at Congress Hall, Clapton. They spoke about their task of covering two million square miles and 300,000,000 inhabitants. Among the pictures shown were: the late King Edward VII on an elephant, a bullock-bandy, a riverboat manoeuvred by a long bamboo pole, and Fakir Singh and Dutini riding on a camel. Cinematograph views were shown of the destruction of a heathen temple and the converts vigorously smashing their long-cherished idols into unrecognisable fragments.

Fakir Singh stated that the S.A. were helping two Aboriginal tribes of the United Provinces – the Bhattus and the Haburahs. He added that a settlement had been formed near to Moradabad where the settlers were being taught weaving, carpentry, agriculture and poultry farming and that the Government of the Punjab had given the S.A. a grant for an industrial settlement. Of 20,000 people in two criminal tribes, only 7,000 had been exempted from the compulsory daily roll-call.

The General Secretary of the S.A. Training College at Clapton considered this Cinematograph service at Congress Hall by Frederick Booth-Tucker to be an exception to the 1909 Cinematograph Act which had prevented the S.A. from exhibiting the Cinematograph in Britain.

Still and Living Pictures were also shown by Booth-Tucker at the Lecture Hall, Eccleston Place at the end of July 1910. The Limelight slides and Cinematograph films were accompanied by the Wandsworth Band. The report in 'The War Cry' makes no distinction between which items were on film or which were photographic Lantern slides. One paragraph stated:- "Converting devil-dancers, turning to Christianity whole villages of people who appealed for S.A. Officers to teach them; demolishing heathen temples, overthrowing idols, nursing the sick, rescuing the fallen, and training the criminal tribes in industries – these were some of the aspects of our work in India".

In an article in 'All the World' from December 1913 Lt. Col. W. Measures talks about the prevalence of devil-worship in the villages in Ceylon:- "When a devil enters a woman she is led to the temple where the priests and devil-dancers are assembled. While the latter are beating tom-toms and singing the woman is beaten with rods, the priests, meanwhile performing certain ceremonies. After becoming hysterical and violent, the woman falls down unconscious, and the devil is said to have been driven out of her. Gifts to the temple and remuneration to the performers complete the business, and the patient is considered to be safe from another attack for several months at least. Among the Estate Tamil coolies, the treatment is less drastic. The woman is taken to a tree and a knot tied in the end of her hair, which is nailed to a tree trunk. A stone is placed on her head, to drive the devil into her hair. This is then cut off, leaving the devil suspended to the tree."

Fakir Singh and Dutini en route for Chauterwa in 1915

In September 1910, "The War Cry" carried an article of an interview with Staff Capt. Diryam (Jackson) about what it was like to run a 'Crim' Settlement:- "Nine months ago I received orders from Comm. Booth-Tucker to open a Settlement among the Sansias, a criminal tribe in the Ludhiana District of the Punjab. Mrs Jackson and I had already spent six months at the Dom settlement studying this special work. On arrival at the nearest station, we rode in an Indian cart two and a half miles through the jungle to the 'Sarai' – a huge fortress, with nearly 140 rooms – which had been placed at the Army's disposal by the Government. The building had been uninhabited for forty years, there were no windows or doors and the whole place was overrun with birds of almost every variety – including wild pigeons, parrots and peacocks – as well as being the home of an equally large number of poisonous snakes, some several feet in length. Here we slept that night! A few days after our arrival the Commissioner of Police brought together the 300 criminals of that district and explained that the S.A. had come among them to help them by teaching them industries to become honest. Through their leaders the people expressed themselves pleased, and we enlisted forty right away. We at once set these to work to clean and repair the building and get the ground ready for seed sowing, and in two months the place was transformed into a veritable palace, surrounded with green fields of barley and wheat and many kinds of vegetables. We had, of course, great difficulty at first in dealing with the people. They did not like work – the majority had done nothing for a living beyond thieving since they were born – and often they would kick over the traces. It took some determination on their part to go straight. One man clearly put the case to me as follows:- "you know how terribly hard it is to stay here. If I went out one night only I could get 500 rupees by thieving." .... The six acres of land which belong to the Settlement had produced crops of turnips, cabbages, peas and tomatoes, which have yielded good returns. ... The carpentry department started with a few men who had absolutely no knowledge of carpentry, but already the work turned out is of high class. Our orders include military butter-boxes; in fact, we turn out all kinds of work from models of bullock carts to seats for Army halls. We also have a dispensary at the settlement which is in the charge of one of our experienced Officers... There are now ninety men, women and children in the Settlement, and weaving, carpentry and gardening are being taught. In the weavery, thirty men are employed. The weavers sit at the looms weaving the cloth for eight hours every day turning out carpet rugs, twill cloth and towels." The editor of 'The War Cry' added that Staff Capt. Jackson had also assisted Brig. Melling in opening a

Settlement for the Pakhiwara criminals of Kot Mohals in the Sialkot district of the Punjab.

After touring Europe Fakir Singh and Dutini left Naples on August 30th 1910 and arrived in Bombay on September 9th. By October 1st they were at Simla where they showed a film depicting their work reclaiming prisoners from the criminal tribes. Their second period in India lasted until June 1914. During this period of almost four years the Government of India had passed their Criminal Tribe Act no. 3.

On returning to India, Dutini became ill and had to return to Britain to recuperate. She subsequently missed the arrival of King George V and Queen Mary to India for the Dhurbar when he was crowned King Emperor on December 12th 1911. Dutini did not return until March 1912.

Following the death of William Booth who was 'Promoted to Glory' at 10.20pm on August 20th 1912, Eva Booth, his daughter, put together, with the assistance of Edward Parker, a Cinematograph and Lantern lecture which she called 'My Father'.

Films were taken by newsreel companies of William Booth's funeral, several of which have survived.

At the end of 1912, two meetings, which the S.A. attended, were held on the subject of the 'White Slave Traffic' at the London Opera House and at the City Temple under the chairmanship of the Archbishop of Canterbury. As a subject 'White Slave Traffic' had been popularised by the Cinematograph from 1907 when the Danish Company Nordisk released "The White Slave". In 1910, the Danish actress Asta Nielson starred in her first film, "Agrafunden" (The Abyss) which became an international success. Many other films on this subject followed, culminating in 1913 with an American production by George Loane Tucker entitled "Traffic in Souls". The arrival in January 1913 of censorship in Britain led to the banning of

William Booth's funeral in 1912

THE SALVATION ARMY AND THE CINEMATOGRAPH 1897 - 1929

Stills taken from various films featuring the funeral of William Booth in 1912 showing the funeral procession from his home to the grave-side and the huge crowds which attended the event as spectators or participants.

THE SALVATION ARMY AND THE CINEMATOGRAPH 1897 - 1929

*Stills from various films featuring the Salvation Army's work in India. Top: Indians from the 'criminal tribes'.
Row 2: "Criminal tribesman" being transferred into the care of the Salvation Army.
Row 3: Indian women being encouraged to remove her jewellery on becoming a Salvationist and children
practice a flower drill. Bottom Row: Commissioner Higgins bids farewell to India in 1905.*

THE SALVATION ARMY,
55 Harrow Road, Paddington Green (near the Edgware Road)

Revival Campaign

Saturday, March 10th, *and Sunday, March 11th,*

COMMISSIONER BOOTH TUCKER

LED BY

Commissioner BOOTH TUCKER

Assisted by the Foreign Office Staff

SATURDAY, at 8 p.m. Subject:

"Lights and Shadows of Salvation Army Warfare in America, India and Japan"

Illustrated by Limelight and Cinematograph Pictures

DRUNKARDS' MARCH AND MIDNIGHT MEETING
Commencing at 11.30

SUNDAY. Subjects:

7 a.m.—"Psalm 23" 3 p.m.—"Where are the Nine?"
11 a.m.—"Nothing but Leaves." 7 p.m.—"Weighed and Found Wanting"

MARYLEBONE BRASS BAND

Special Features! New and Beautiful Revival Songs from America and Sweden . . .

ADMISSION FREE (except on Saturday)
LECTURE with LIMELIGHT and CINEMATOGRAPH, 3d.

1906 Revival Campaign led by Commissioner Booth-Tucker with cinematograph presentation on 'Lights and Shadows of Salvation Army Warfare in America, India and Japan'

films which dealt with white slavery, prostitution and suicide – all of which shared a common link. The S.A. had set up an Anti-suicide bureau as well as opening Rescue Homes for those women who had been caught in 'the white slavery trap'. An article in "The War Cry" of January 1914 stated:- "White Slavers are not exclusively white men. There is a growing practice for Orientals to come to European countries, and by all manner of alluring devices, entice respectable young women to the Orient, where they are forced into an evil life. In almost every case a promise of marriage is held out to, or a form of marriage is undergone with the victim.... There is a fearful amount of traffic in woman-hood carried on between the Dutch East Indies and Singapore, and 'The Army' is about to open a special Rescue and Preventative home in that part to combat the evil.... After 3pm each week-day and on every Sunday, Malay Street in Singapore is one of the sights of the East. It is the great gaudy centre of the Babylonian Quarter where thousands of prostitutes of every nationality under the sun congregate on the verandas of the houses and openly solicit the passers-by. The broad open verandas are of stone and are raised stage-like some three feet from the roadway. On them the women pose in easy chairs or on carpets, smoking cigarettes, laughing, chatting and accosting each passer-by... over 500 of these dens are centred in and about Malay Street, each house containing 8 to 25 girls, and as the death rate is heavy, the great army of procurers is necessarily kept busy. Many of the dens are very unsafe to enter, murder and robbery being very common occurrences, while death certificates are cheap." During 1915, Henry Howse had produced a Cinematograph film entitled "Meg of the Slums", starring Helena Millais. In the film she is enticed into 'white slavery' before being rescued.

During 1913 Mayor Ishwar Das compiled a new set of Lantern slides regarding the S.A. work in India. These were included in the S.A.'s 1914 Magic Lantern Catalogue. He also shot several moving pictures including 'The Muktipur Colony'. Fakir Singh began adopting the scheme which he had worked on during the period he had spent in the USA with the Native Indian Reservations.

Other films which Ishwar Das assembled, dealt with the Industrial Exhibition for criminal workers; the opening of the Thomas Emery hospital at Moradabad by Lt. Gov. James Meeston, and the opening of the new Rescue Homes in Madras by Lady Pentland. Seventy three S.A. Officers, including Capt. Ellen Olsen from Sweden who arrived in India in 1914, were recruited around this time for the Indian 'battlefield' and also for a leper colony which the S.A. had established in Java. There were 50,000 lepers in the Dutch East Indies.

The following are examples of films that Fakir Singh and Dutini presented between 1910 and 1914 (before they returned to Britain for the Int. S.A. Congress in London).

1910

In the Autumn of 1910, Fakir Singh began regular open air meetings on The Ridge at Simla. Films that were shown included the 'Funeral of King Edward VII'. However, 'The Life of Christ' remained their main attraction. At the Masonic Hall in Simla, he showed a film depicting the work of the S.A. amongst the criminal classes. This was probably filmed by Major Ishwar Das who had also returned from Europe with them in 1910.

At the Railway Institute at Gorakhpur, film of the 'The Naval Review at Spithead' was shown. At Bombay, a volley of shots from the cadets announced the arrival of Fakir Singh and Dutini. Again a film of the criminal settlements in North India and the Punjab was presented.

1911

At Simla, around Easter 1911, Fakir Singh gave a lecture at the Gaiety Theatre on the subject of Social Reclamation by the Salvation Army. Dutini presented herself as a living representation of the

Filming at the 1914 Congress at the Crystal Palace

'Madonna of the Slums', the story of which was set in the Klondyke. 5,000 were present at Simla Ridge to celebrate the Coronation of King George V. One film that was shown was of the Reception in Calcutta of the Viceroy of India, Lord and Lady Hardinge which had been filmed by Major Ishwar Das. The Viceroy and his wife were in the congregation on the hillside when the film was shown.

1912

A film was shown at the S.A. hall in Simla of 'The Delhi Dhurbar' as well as 'A Railway journey through the mountains of Switzerland'. At Simla Ridge the S.A. charged 4 or 2 annas each for those who were sitting near to Fakir Singh with his megaphone. Surrounding these were a second group, behind which were those who were non-Christians.

At Gorakhpur where the S.A. had been working with the Dommara tribe for the past four years, Fakir Singh visited the Bazaar with a megaphone. A screen was set up in the centre of a large market place. Approximately 6,000 attended the lecture which included a film of the Nagercoil school boys bathing in the river. The Cinematograph screen was viewed from both sides.

At Bartola in December 1912, 5,000 attended an open air service on 'The Life of Christ' – "First a weeping woman made her way to the sheet and at the foot, where she had seen reflected the image and suffering of our Lord, threw herself upon the ground to be His and His alone. Perhaps one hundred and fifty followed her."

Much of the travelling that Fakir Singh had to do – by train, car, boat, elephant, horse and bullock had taken its toll on his health. This resulted in the HQ at Simla becoming the main outlet for their lectures.

A book review of "The Light of India" by Harold Begbie in the Journal "All The World" (April 1913) included a description of a visit by Begbie to some imprisoned 'Doms' :- "They were dressed for the most part in awkward, thick, hairy coats of dark grey, edged with white, and wore from a steel ring circling their necks a block of wood stamped with the dates of their sentences and the Act under which they had been convicted. Two or three had steel gyves upon their ankles, but the majority wore only a single ring on one leg, to which the full fetters would be attached when there was any danger of escape. They were squatting on their haunches, the arms laid across the knees, the heads inclining wearily in every case towards one of the humped shoulders. Upon their shaven heads was a small round cap – foul, greasy and worn at as many different angles as there were prisoners."

Filming at the 1914 Congress at the Crystal Palace

A further extract from Begbie's book was given in 'The War Cry' in April 1914. "Should a person fall sick, and the devil-dancer failed to get rid of Dakan (an extremely malignant female devil), who has caused the illness, a Bhil family will move their hut – perhaps a whole village will move – in order to escape the haunting spirit. Death itself is attributed to this devil. A person would never die but for the enmity of Dakan. Some spirit of good is supposed to preside over human life, probably Mata, the Earth Mother, and when a person dies, the Bhil says that the Devil has triumphed over this good spirit."

This same article in "The War Cry" in April 1914 also included an extract from the latest "India's Cry" in which Brig. Jang Bahadur (Winge) talks about his works amongst the Bhils. 'The Brig. is the owner of three small tents which are pitched on an open ground, with the flag of the S.A. flying from a high pole in the centre. His stock in trade consists of a gramophone with about 100 records, a capital Lantern with a very powerful light and a large number of slides. Two bullock-carts are requisitioned to carry the luggage, and everything necessary for camping out for 4 or 5 months…… "We were provided with horses to ride, and our programme each day was somewhat as follows:- an hour before sunrise we rose and dressed, and found tea and toast ready to our hands. Mounting our horses we rode out from 3 to 7 miles to where it had been previously announced we should be conducting a meeting. Soon after our arrival the converts began to gather, although few, if any, houses might be in sight. By means of a megaphone they could often be called, and whatever might have been the means of letting them know, we soon had from 10 to 30 people to talk to.... The meeting over, we would ride to another centre, where the same thing would be repeated. This allowed us to go back to the camp about 12 o'clock midday.... At 3 o'clock in the afternoon a mother's and children's meeting might be announced ... then at night as soon as it was dark, a large sheet was erected, a table brought out and a gramophone requisitioned. When a crowd had gathered, the Lantern was used, illustrating phases of Army work in this country, Old Testament scripture, as well as the life of Christ..... This kind of work is done by the Brig. for nearly five months of the year (not for the wet and very hot seasons).'"

In "All The World" for April 1913 Brig. Hunter (Bahadur) described his work at Gorakhpur where he and his wife had charge of 300 'Doms'.... "The day a child is born to a Dom mother it's name is scheduled on the list of criminals, and there it remains until the end of its life. The ordinary Dom tribesman with his dependents is locked in at night by the police and liberated in the morning... If he is missing at night, he is arrested and imprisoned ... a tribesman who stole a brass vessel and some food, valued at 2 rupees 2 annas (about 2s.8d.) ... was sentenced to 21 years imprisonment and sent to Port Blair Convict settlement on the Andaman Islands."

In October 1913, Mrs Hunter also wrote an article for "All The World" concerning 'The First Criminal Settlement'. One paragraph stated:- " About sunset each evening of every week the unfortunate creatures were hustled into their enclosures, then the roll would be called, the large gate locked with a key which was kept at the nearest police-station until daybreak. Sometimes during the night a surprise visit would be made and the roll would be called... if the owner of any name on that roll was absent, their name would be reported ... he would be imprisoned for being out after hours without a pass."

An article entitled "India – Fifty 'Good' Doms" which appeared in "The War Cry" in January 1914 included extracts from a letter received from Capt. Wuah Sagar (Johnson);- " The S.A. Criminal Settlement Gorakhpur, now under the supervision of Adj. Dana Das and Dana Bai (Adj. and Mrs. Pimm Smith) has largely extended its borders during the last few months. The latest increase is the arrival of a party of 50 Doms – 15 men and 35 women and children from a village 36 miles away. Of the men, four were old and one was dumb. The eleven able-bodied men walked the 36 miles. They were handcuffed and also roped together. The remainder of the party came with their luggage on bullock-carts... When the people had been handed over to us and the papers signed, the police escort, 136 strong, was reviewed by an inspector. In this Settlement now we have nearly 500 Doms but such is the hold of the Muktifauj (Salvation Army) upon them that our total staff including that for the school for Dom children, is now seven European Officers (3 of the late Memorial party), one Singalese, one native Officer, three Settlement masters, two Industrial masters, and two teachers – only 16 in all. Compare this staff for 500 Doms with the 136 police officials required to bring the 50 to us, and you will see at once the wonderful influence which is exercised by the S.A. over these people."

During 1914, Col. Henry Bullard wrote a number of articles in S. A. journals about his visit to India over a two-month period. He had been part of the original pioneer party led by Comm. Booth-Tucker to India in 1883. In one of his articles he wrote:- "At Gorakhpur, the prison is a great high-walled enclosure looking from the exterior like a great fort. Inside, the buildings are in rows, and all on the ground level... here we have settled 250 of the Dom tribe ... some of these are daily employed in the city, nevertheless they still live in the settlement under our supervision. For others we find employment making carpets, towels, weaving cloth, and reeling silk.... At Moradabad, a very large bungalow and the adjoining grounds have been placed at our disposal; also a large tract of land in the suburbs of the city, on which an enclosed settlement has been erected. Here we have 300 of the Haburah's tribe. ... At Aligarth we have a large fort, with huge high walls and a deep moat surrounding it. The only entrance is by a drawbridge and tunnelled gateway. The interior of the fort is simply a great flat area, and at the time we took over the occupancy it contained only a couple of large bungalows. Within this fort we have erected an enclosed settlement for 300 of the Beriah's tribe. Some are employed on the erection of a Mohammedan College in the neighbourhood of the

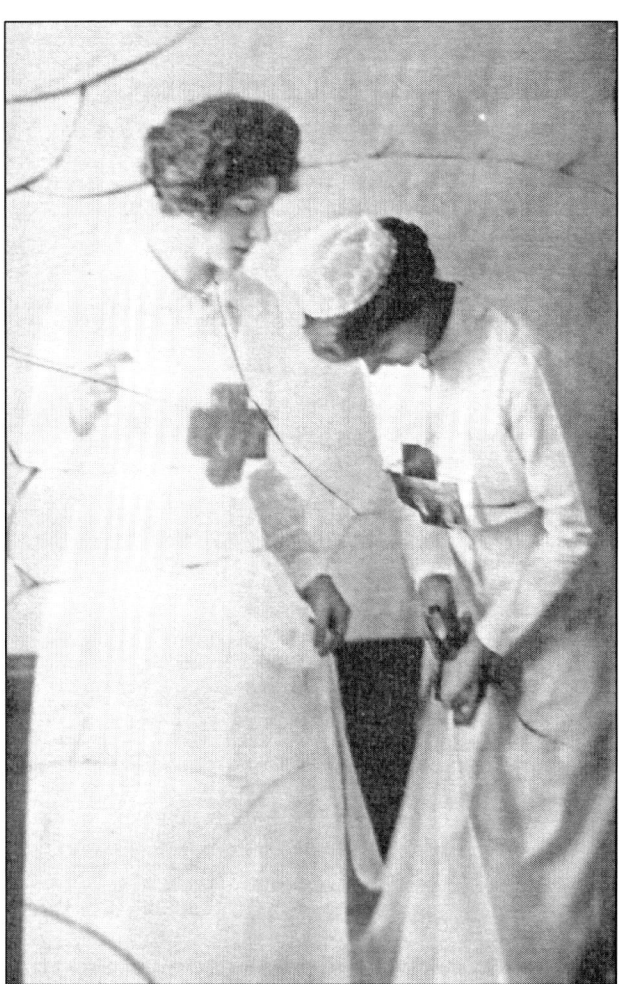

THE SALVATION ARMY AND THE CINEMATOGRAPH 1897 - 1929

Lantern slides produced during the Great War

Salvation Army march through Trafalgar Square during the 1914 Congress in London

fort, and others are occupied weaving, mat making, and silk reeling... At Chawa we have a fort very similar where work of the same nature is in progress for the Sansiah tribe. In addition, we have settlements at Kanth, Sahibgary, Keshipur and Bareilly, in the United Provinces; also at Belliah i Behar, and Orissa, and there are others scattered about in different parts of India. The Salvation Army advertised that their message of Christ was proclaimed in the native languages of the Punjabis, Guzeratis, Mahrattas, Bhils, Telegus, Tamils, Malayalis and Cingalese."

Col. Bullard also wrote about the S.A. work among the lower castes or 'palayahs'. He stated that until recently a low caste woman was not allowed to wear any covering about her waist. He also stated that the palayahs are nearly all agriculturalists and are usually employed by the Sudras, an influential and wealthy section of the high caste. At Travancore, he wrote that:- " Our Officers register births, conduct dedications, perform marriage ceremonies and conduct the funerals. We have our own school and our own cemeteries."

At Nagercoil the S.A. ran the Catherine Booth Hospital under Dr. (Maj) Percy Turner. Bullard also wrote about the practice of conversion stating:- "after enrolment, the village temple and idols will be destroyed, they will abandon their heathen practices, and place themselves under us for spiritual instruction."

During Fakir Singh and Dutini's stay in London in June 1914 for the International Congress, they also attended a missionary conference for S.A. Officers from India, Java, Japan, Korea and Africa. The Congress itself had been marred by the loss of life of one hundred and thirty three Officers who were travelling to London from Canada on 'The Empress of Ireland' which foundered in the St. Lawrence River.

During their third tour of duty (1914- 1917) Fakir Singh and Dutini had taken over responsibility for Burma in addition to India and Ceylon. (However, their health had begun to suffer and Dutini was again forced to return to Britain for an extended break.) In an article in "All The World" at the beginning of 1917, Adj. Gulab Bai wrote about the development in Burma as follows: - "The first company of prisoners has already been received. They came in the prison-van with an armed escort. At the gates of the home they were handed over to the care of our Officers, who are now responsible for them. The prison garb has been replaced by smart 'lungyis', jackets, and silk head gear... Their day begins at 6am with coffee and bread and butter; after this, prayers are led by the

Officers; then follows work, with regular intervals for food and recreation; 9.45pm lights out." Burma was different from India since there were no criminal tribes. Instead the S.A. cared for habitual criminals.

In Britain, the S.A. regulations had been tightened up on the use of the Cinematograph. Approval would now be required from the highest level for its use.

However, Fakir Singh continued to use the Cinematograph but more sparingly, instead Lantern slides began to dominate his lectures. In Britain, Florence Booth (Bramwell Booth's wife) and Col. Unsworth had been concerned about the moral effect of the Cinematograph on children. She was a member of the National Union of Women Workers and had given her views both to the Home Office and the L.C.C. Education Department. With a group of S.A. Officers she had interviewed children who had attended film shows. She reported that the only comedies that children liked were those featuring Charlie Chaplin. She singled out one unidentified film for criticism in which the heroine lures three young men to a gambling den, wrecking their lives. She also commented negatively on a number of films that covered the war in Europe, remarking that, "they displayed the animal lust for destruction". In 1918 'The Officer' stated that the vows taken by S.A. Officers ran counter to their attending Cinematograph Halls.

During the penultimate period of their charge of India (1914-17), I've singled out three references on the use of the Cinematograph and the hardships which they encountered. Early in 1916 they had to travel 90 miles in three days between Trivandrum and Tiruvella. The party of ten journeyed in three vellums – flat-bottomed boats covered with palm leaves, over a series of lakes and canals. In Moradabad, in order to advertise the Cinematograph service, two Officers with handbills and a boy with a kettle drum were sent to stir up other parts of the city to attend the service. A reference was made to a fiction film being shown in one of the cinemas in Gujerat which depicted a 'dilapidated' individual who attends an S.A. meeting, is saved, restores the property he has stolen and becomes a Salvationist.

During 1917, Fakir Singh and Dutini had found it difficult to return to Britain in time to attend the wedding of one of his daughters as well as participate in a conference on India's problems presided over by Lord Sydenham. It took them seventy days to reach Britain, rather than the usual seventeen and they only

Salvation Army hospital at Moradabad taken over for war wounded

The dangers of cinema-going for the young

THE SALVATION ARMY AND THE CINEMATOGRAPH 1897 - 1929

Open-air lecture by Fakir Singh

remained for two months. In letters sent to the "War Cry" (India) they gave details of the difficulties which they had encountered journeying to Britain on the Trans-Siberian route. Fakir Singh and Dutini arrived back at Simla early in 1918. They returned via Canada and Japan. The 17,000 mile journey to Colombo took over two months and before they reached their HQ at Simla they had to travel a further 2,000 miles by rail.

Their health again had suffered due to the continuous travelling difficulties that they had endured. During 1918 Famine and Plague took hold in India. They remained in India until May 1919 when they both returned to Britain on sick leave. It seems that Booth-Tucker had suffered a stroke which affected his speech.

Later that year they both resigned their posts. Most of their final appearances had been at Simla particularly on the Ridge where thousands gathered to hear Fakir Singh's lecture on 'The Life of Christ'. After their departure the combined film and Lantern slide lectures were continued for a period by Major Ishwar Das and Ensign Nur Das, who projected the films and Lantern slides for "Bioscope Nights on the Ridge" where seating, (on a chair), cost 4 annas.

Fakir Singh's final period in India (1918/19) had been marred by the return of famine, the influenza epidemic and rioting.

An article by Col. Joshua Spooner (Balwant) in "All The World" in June 1920 stated:- "The complete failure of the 1918 monsoon in Western India resulted in terrible famine conditions throughout the latter half of 1918. A Bombay Famine Relief Committee was set up:- 'The Wadier Charitier' came forward with a gift of 10,000 rupees for the wells, the sinking of which gave employment to 600 famine sufferers.... which enabled us to grow fodder for the starving cattle." Col. Spooner went on to ask the readers of "All The World" for donations in order to sink 'Memorial wells' stating that each will irrigate 12 acres. By the following summer Spooner himself had died.

Fakir Singh had sent a letter to Bramwell Booth describing "the sad picture of children wandering in the jungle in search of berries and roots". The food prices had shot up and Fakir Singh had suggested the cultivation of cactus in order to feed cattle during famine periods.

Epidemics of cholera, the plague and influenza were widespread. A number of S.A. Officers, including nurses, had died at Ahmedabad.

From

INDIA'S CORAL STRAND

A Cinematograph Tour through the Indian Empire

Reviewing the activities of The Salvation
:: Army in that fascinating land ::

INDIA ◊ CEYLON ◊ BURMA
*All the Principal Cities
and Places of Interest*

In July 1919 "All The World" had reported that serious rioting had taken place probably due to the effects of the famine. At Amritsar, Europeans had been attacked in their offices and clubbed to death. The S.A. were concerned about the safety of their staff at Lahore, but decided not to relocate. Fakir Singh probably realised that what India now needed to carry on the work of the S.A. was a much younger group of men and women Officers with the drive, energy and good health which he himself now lacked.

Bramwell Booth visited India for two weeks at the end of 1922 and early 1923, possibly as part of the preparation for the British Empire Exhibition to be held at Wembley in 1925. The S.A. put on an Indian theatre production during the exhibition. Nessie Tucker later recalled:- "There was one (scene) where a young man had a poisoned foot and the Devil Dancer was sent for and performed his rites to the accompaniment of weird music. The patient became worse and then a Christian Indian teacher arrived, extracted a thorn from his foot (with a pen-knife) and the boy recovered and the family became Christian." During 1925, Henry Howse also visited India to make a film for the Missionary Film Committee which was called "India To-day". In "The War Cry" (India) (July 1925) there is a reference to Howse journeying to India with his wife, Brig. Deva Ratna and Yudha Prakas when they visited Nagercoil. "India To-day" opened at the Polytechnic in London in September 1925. Howse had shot 28,000ft. of film which had been reduced to

Do not miss seeing
KHUSHI AND HER GIRLS
They will appear with the wonderful
:: Eastern Film ::
"FROM INDIA'S CORAL STRAND"
At
THE PUMP ROOM
THE PANTILES, TUNBRIDGE WELLS
Monday and Tuesday
September 20th and 21st, 1926
Three Times Daily at 3.0, 5.30 and 8.0 p.m.

POPULAR PRICES

Haycock, Cadle & Graham Ltd. Camberwell, S.E.5.

Advertising postcard for film show at Tunbridge Wells in 1926

Khushi and her girls who accompanied the film

two sections of 5,000ft.each.

Whether there is any link between Howse's visit to India and the S.A.'s own independent film "From India's Coral Strand" has yet to be determined. Frederick Cox was summoned out of retirement by Comm. Higgins (chief of staff) to help manage the film's distribution. Cox stated that the film was made by W.L. Devoto and was not an S.A. film. However, Devoto was a bandsman who in 1926 emigrated with his family to the USA. I have found no link between him and the making of the film apart from Cox's reference in the Biographical notes by Cox's son. Devoto may have been involved with the musical aspects of the film along with Ellen Olsen (Khushi) who had arrived in Britain with a party of eight girls from the Satara Girls School, who were to accompany the film. Olsen had gone to India in 1914 as part of the 'Memorial Party'. She was originally from Karlshamn in Sweden and her musical speciality was giving a nightingale solo. The film was to be shown in public halls rather than cinemas, but not in S.A. Citadels (according to Cox). However, between January and March 1927 the film was shown in S.A. Citadels, although Cox stated that S.A. uniforms were not to be worn. Cox also said that the film proved not to be a financial success. Its aim had been to raise funds for the S.A. work in India and Ceylon. It is possible that this film could have included sections from some earlier films that were made by Mjr. Glanville (Ishwar Das) between 1910 – 1914, together with some

THE SALVATION ARMY AND THE CINEMATOGRAPH 1897 - 1929

THE WAR CRY, March 19, 1910

WITH THE GENERAL'S BIRTHDAY NUMBER, APRIL 9th—A LOVELY PLATE FREE OF COST

THE WAR CRY

OFFICIAL GAZETTE OF THE SALVATION ARMY

INTERNATIONAL HEADQUARTERS, [Registered at the General Post Office as a Newspaper.] 101 QUEEN VICTORIA STREET

No. 1,756]   LONDON, SATURDAY, MARCH 19, 1910   [PRICE ONE PENNY

'FROM INDIA'S CORAL STRAND'

The film's title has been used on many occasions by the Salvation Army including this one from 1910

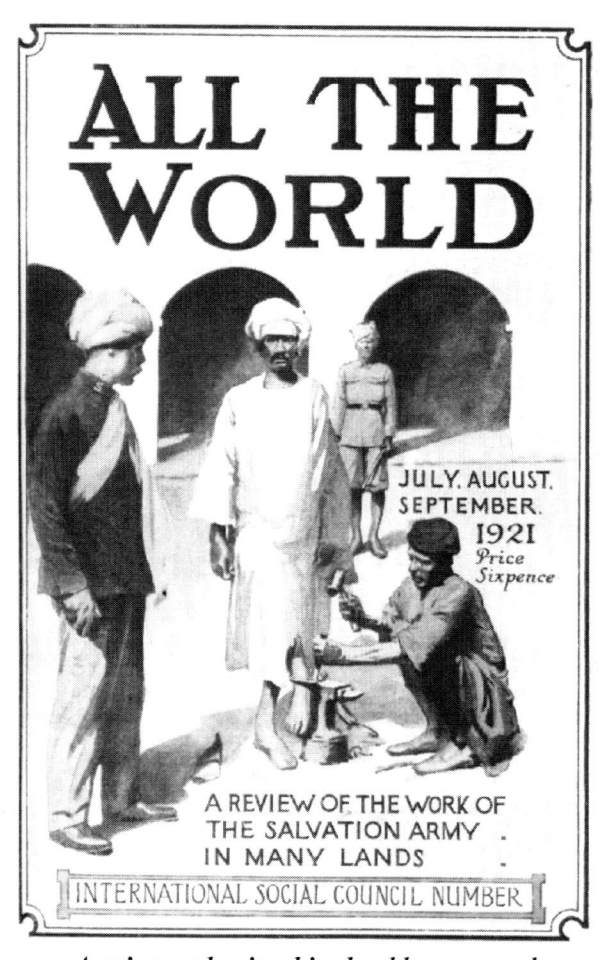

A prisoner having his shackles removed

later re-created sections by Howse or others. The Salvation Army probably distanced themselves from the film because of their own reluctance to admit that they had produced it while their own regulations remained hostile to any such project.

The film was first circulated in September 1926 and the booklet 'Salvation Army Missionary Work in India' was issued to accompany the film's brochure entitled 'From India's Coral Strand'. Lt. Comm. Edgar Hoe was in charge of the film's exhibition. As Hira Singh, he had returned to India in December 1925 to give lectures on the S.A. work there. He remained until the end of June 1926.

A new arrival at a criminal settlement

He had originally served in India in 1889 accompanied by his wife, Amrita Bai (Polly Burgess). He had also worked there between 1918 - 1923 following Fakir Singh's resignation.

During the 1926 tour of Great Britain, they visited a 'darkened' hall in Colchester in which Khushi and her girls sang 'For India, there's a Saviour' and 'Loving Me as He Loves You', as part of their accompaniment to the film. Frederick Cox recalled that he had booked one hundred halls for the tour over an eight month period. The poster advertising the film featured Fakir Singh (Booth-Tucker) with the S.A. flag welcoming groups of Indians - he is remembered by the S.A. as being 'the Apostle of India'.

The film included a Buddhist temple in Rangoon; the Bhils (one of the criminal tribes the S.A. worked with); an S.A. Corps in Gujerat; the Catherine Booth Memorial Hospital and its work and settlers harvesting their crops at Shantinagar. Certain sequences in the film were re-created specifically for the Cinematograph, such as the sequence of eating raw meat and cooking a baby leopard. One lengthy intertitle stated "Nomadic and gypsy-like inhabitants, the criminal tribes of India constitute a continual menace to society, a terror to the police, and a problem to the government. Their hand is against every man and every man's hand is against them. Social parasites, they exist by robbery, theft, burglary, blackmail and even murder. They are highly organised, independent and fearless – numbering one and a half million. The problem of their reform is being tackled by the government on broad, magnanimous lines, in a statesman like manner. In this work, the S.A. has pledged an important part, having under it's care about 8,000 people of the tribes."

Part of the reason for the film's distribution was that the S.A. needed funds to help to establish a new criminal settlement in the Andaman Islands which opened in June 1927. This was a two-year experiment at Kala Pam with settlers from the United Provinces.

PROGRAMME

PART I.
The Emblem of the British Empire.

CEYLON.

Ratnapoora.
The City of Rubies—A Village Street—The Mine, with its Shafts—Washing, Cutting and Polishing the Jewels—A Gorgeous Display.

A Country Road.
Turning the Roadbed, with Traffic continued.

Kandy.
The Mountains, Gardens, Markets, Porters and People.

Anaradapoora.
The First Capital of Ceylon, with its Buddhist Remains.

Religious Procession.
Embracing the Sacred Elephants, with the Native Dances, etc.

The Canal.
With banks lined with palms.

A Fishing Village.
Bustling with activity.

Village Beauties.
Agreeable and contented.

The Catamoran.
Strange boats with strange ideas.

Rameswaram.
A Holy City.

Madura.
Old Temples culled from a collection at Jagenath, Madras and Madura, with Tamil types as well.

Trichinopoly.
The Mountain Temple.

Goa.
A Beautiful Country, with its Salt Industry.

Bombay.
A combination of contrasts, human and architectural.

Nasik.
The Western Benares—Shoeing Bullock, Quaint Market and the Goat Herd.

Jeypore.
A Modern City, with many improvements but no real Native life.

Amber.
The Ruined City—A Casket of Mountain Gems deserted by man.

Ulwar.
A Resting Place.

The Road to Delhi.
Strange Road Traffic—The Cashmere Gate—Chandni Chauk—Friday Mosque—Inside Fort—Two Famous Tombs—The Ancient City, with Ruins of the First Mosque—St. James's Church—General John Nicholson—The Army in Being.

Cawnpore.
The Memorial Church and Tablets—The Temple of Siva—Memorial Gardens—The Well—The Cross.

FINISH OF PART I.

An Oriental Interlude.

Mrs. R. G. Knowles

introduces her Wonderful Collection of Eastern Costumes.

Most Unique—A Glorious Blaze of Colour and Oriental Magnificence.

This, together with the Decorations used in the Hall, is her Sole Property and was selected by her during the "World Tour" of Mr. and Mrs. R. G. Knowles.

PART II.

Allahabad.
With its Gateway, Streets, Public School, Mayo Memorial—Statue and Tomb of Prince Khusru.

Magh Mela.
The Great Hindoo Festival—at the Junction of the Jumna and the Ganges.

Gwalior.
The Fort—Rock Carvings—The Palace and Surbar Drawing Room.

Agra.
Street in Agra—Women at Well—Native Builders and the Life Story of Shah Jehan depicted in Marble, with his Culminating Triumph, the Taj Mahal.

Benares.
The most famous of all the Holy Cities—Temples, Mosques and Palaces—The Snake Charmer.

Calcutta.
The Hugli with its Bridge and Shipping.

The Mohurrum.
The Mohammedan Festival.

The Viceroy's Cup.
A Study in Faces.

North of the Hugli.
A Quiet Stroll after the Hurly Burly which leads us to the

Jain Temple.
A most Wonderful Creation, with Incense Burners and Shrines.

The Review of the Elephants.
A most Wonderful Gathering of the most Intelligent Animals on Earth.

The Mountains of Himalaya.
Up in the Ice and Snow—The Actual Top of the World.

A kinemacolor tour of India by R G Knowles 1914

After the 1926/27 exhibition the film was shown by the S.A. in Congress Hall, Clapton in February 1928 and several lengthy sections survive today at the BFI. A list of the venues where the film was shown is included in the Addendum.

Just before the film went on tour an article appeared in "The International Review of Missions" in April 1926 by Dora Tickell. She had been a member of the SPG (Society for the Preservation of the Gospel) Ahmednagar Mission for thirteen years, during which period she had spent some time working at a criminal tribe settlement at Hubli. Part of her interview appeared in "All The World" in October 1926, in which she writes about the S.A. work with the 'criminal tribes':-
"In north India the Salvation Army Settlements are dealing principally with the Bhattus, Sansiahs (cattle thieves), Doms, Haburahs, (beggars and pickpockets) and Khasbands. Of these, they tell us that the Bhatus seem to be the most desperate tribe, often committing dacoity with murder, while the Sansiahs are said to settle down far better than most other tribes.... (the Erukahs/Korchas in the Telegu territory) live a nomadic life generally, travelling with cattle and often annexing the village cattle as they pass through. In the past they have probably been legitimate carriers and traders of salt, grain, and other necessaries. Mat and basket-making are also among their occupations. Some have settled on the outskirts of village life, acting as village musicians and playing at weddings, while others live entirely in the jungle. But among these sub-divisions of the caste there appears to be evidence of a strong criminal organisation... the women of the tribe, who combine fortune-telling with selling baskets give valuable help in gathering and passing on information .... The work of the Salvation Army in their settlements in North and South India is far better known to the general public than that of other missions engaged with criminal tribes.... The industrial and evangelistic sides of their work would appear to be more prominent than the educational."

Above: Filmstrip of 'From India's Coral Strand' of a group of lace makers

Below: Lantern slide of leper victims in Java

In March 1926 Bramwell Booth celebrated his 70th birthday with a Lantern presentation on his life shown at the Royal Albert Hall, with his son, Bernard, as lecturer.

On September 18th 1926, Bramwell left for a visit of Japan. On reaching Canada he heard the news of the death of his younger brother, Herbert, in Yonkers, New York. Their sister, Eva, had been present at the death.

Bramwell's reason for visiting Japan may have been due to a Bill which the Japanese Parliament was considering. The proposal would only allow persons to speak in public who had received fourteen years education in Japan. This would have restricted S.A. Officers from Britain from their work. This proposal was later amended to effect only those people who earned their living by speaking in public.

Bramwell's visit also coincided with the transfer of the S.A. leadership in Japan from Comm. Eadie

SALVATIONIST PUBLISHING & SUPPLIES, LTD.

Modern Miracles in India
(Set No. 5a)

1. Commissioner Fakir Singh.
2. S.A. Headquarters for India, Simla.
3. The Kaiser-i-Hind Medal.
4. 'Little Thin-armed Women.'
5. Parsees.
6. Children with Caste Marks.
7. Native Street, India.
8. A Native Baker.
9. The Village Well.
10. Indian Gods.
11. Vullums on Backwaters.
12. Villages on Backwaters.
13. Mohammedan Muharram.
14. S.A. Officers on the March.
15. Part of the Crowd in the Pandal.
16. Another View of the Crowd.
17. Boys' Band.
18. Girls Drilling.
19. Boys Drilling.
20. The Penitents.
21. The Final Consecration.
22. Arms Full of Live Fowls.
23. A Devil Dancer, now Salvationist.
24. The Witch.
25. Actually Worshipped before Her.
26. 'The Saint of Manady.'
27. East Vadasery Village.
28. Massilamony and Family.
29. Threshing Floor, Turned Temple.
30. Break-up of Temple.
31. Smashing the Idol.
31A. Benares: Palaces and Temples.
31B. Benares: River's Edge and Pilgrims.
32. Household Idols.
33. 'Bhisti' with Dripping Goatskin.
34. A Snake Charmer.
35. Emaciated and Filthy Saint.
36. Corpse prepared for Burial.
37. Enormous Bull.
38. Temple Monkeys.
39. A Fakir.
40. Fakir suspended from Tree.
41. Ceylon: Mountain and Forest.
42. Journey by Bullock-cart.

LANTERN SLIDE DEPARTMENT

Modern Miracles in India
(Set No. 5b)

43. Procession of Salvationists.
44. Mud Houses.
45. Eating Curry and Rice.
46. Cingalese Men.
47. Brigadier Samaraveera.
48. Ceylon Rescue Home.
49. Street in Colombo.
50. A Bhil Headman and his Wife.
51. A Criminal Settlement.
52. A Sikh Warder.
53. Visit to Doms in Prison.
54. The Captain of a Gang of Dacoits.
55. A Hangman.
56. Weaving Looms.
57. A Weaving Shed in Criminal Settlement.
58. Some of the Criminal Men.
59. Some of the Criminal Women.
60. Chawa Criminal Settlement.
61. A Sansia Woman: Criminal Tribe.
62. A Sansia Man: A famous Wrestler.
63. Sansia Woman doing Lace Work.
64. A Colony of one-time Criminals.
65. More of the Colonists.
66. We Teach them Silkworm Culture.
67. Manager's House, Tati.
68. Silkworms on Trays.
69. Winding Silk for Looms.
70. Boy with Silk made at Settlement.
71. Criminal Children at Army School.
72. One of our Teachers.
73. Cattle of the Jungle Villagers.
74. Hospital Work.
75. A Famine Victim.
76. Child Rescued from Famine.
77. Reinforcements for India.
78. Indian Party with Dom Criminal Children.
79. Leaving I.H.Q. for March through London.
80. Through Fleet Street.
81. In the West End.
82. Entering Euston Station.
83. Ensign Isa Das, a Brahmin Devotee.

SALVATIONIST PUBLISHING & SUPPLIES, LTD.

Salvation Army Work Abroad
MISSIONARY LECTURE
(Set No. 8)

RED INDIANS (Alaska, Canada)
1. Half civilized Indian at a potlach (feast).
2. Totem pole, with idol on top.
3. Salvation Army Corps at Port Essington, Alaska.
4. Port Essington, the town.
5. Glen Vowell, An Army Settlement with the Citadel, and part of the village built by Native Salvationists in the centre.
6. An Army funeral at Port Simpson, another Settlement.

SOUTH AFRICA
7. Group of Zulus having a meal of porridge out on the veld.
8. On the way to Zululand—our Officer's wagon crossing Tugela River.
9. Zulu Kraals—see huts inside kraal fences, on hillside.
10. One of the huts in a kraal. An old man's youngest wife (of seven) and her family.
11. Zulu warriors. A Chief trying a prisoner.
12. A Royal Chief.
13. Zulu married women.
14. When the women marry they do their hair into a top knot like this.
15. Zulu lads—showing native bead work decorations.
16. Mashona girls. The women do all the menial work and the men are mostly idle.
17. Women bringing water from the river on our Pearson Settlement, Matabeleland, Rhodesia.
18. How the women carry children.
19. Men preparing a skin for loin cloth.
20. In the towns the men draw rickshaws and decorate themselves with horns.
21. Our first Zulu Convert—now Adjutant M'Bambo—with Major Marcus.
22. Typical Zulu Corps.
23. General view of buildings on an Army Settlement—School-house to the left.
24. An open-air school class.
25. Boys and girls at school together.
26. A sewing class outside.
27. First batch of Mashona Cadets sent into Native Work.
28. South African native 'War Cry,' published monthly.

JAPAN
29. Japan—the land of the cherry blossom. Garden of well-to-do family.
30. A Japanese Corps.
31. Open-Air Meeting, Tokio.
32. Hall and Quarters, Tokio.
33. A Corps of Juniors, Osaka.
34. Japanese Rescue Home.
35. Army Home for Students, at the University.
36. Major Beaumont and Japanese Cadets.
37. The General in a Rickshaw (Commissioner Higgins and Colonel Bullard).

JAVA
38. Group of Javanese peasants.
39. Street market in Semarang, the Capital.

LANTERN SLIDE DEPARTMENT

Missionary Work—continued

41. Our Headquarters at Semarang.
42. European and Native Officers.
43. Group of afflicted people handed over to The Army.
44. The Patients in our Industrial Settlement at Boenganger, Java.

KOREA
45. Korean ladies.
46. In Seoul, the Capital; bringing firewood into the city.
47. A Korean basket maker.
48. Natives pounding rice.
49. Officers' Quarters and Hall at Song Dong.
50. Group of Korean Local Officers.
51A. Korean Juniors of Seoul I Corps.
51B. Korean Cadets.
52. Korean Officers and Soldiers.

WEST INDIAN ISLANDS
53. Typical scene among the islands, Port Maria.
54. Jamaica Natives.
55. On the way to market.
56. Quite a swell! Bermuda boy.
57. Officers' Quarters, Pelican Island, Trinidad.
58. After the earthquake, Port Antonio.
59. The Army on the march, Kingston, Jamaica; Colonel Maidment in front.
60. Officers of the West Indies.

INDIA
61. Commissioner Fakir Singh (Booth-Tucker).
62. Indian Headquarters.
63. Indian children, see caste marks on forehead.
64. Indian gods.
65. Village in Ceylon.
66. An Indian meal.
67. Divisional Officer's Quarters and Office, Ceylon.
68. Indian Fakir or holy man.
69. Sacred bull in the streets.
70. Famine children from Industrial School, drilling.
71. Band of Native Training Garrison, Travancore.
72. A Boom March—Colonel Sukh Singh in front.
73. Criminal Tribes—Group of Bhils with bows and arrows.
74. Bhil women.
75. Doms, 'loutish men and tigerish women.' (See 'Light of India.')
76. A Criminal Settlement—Port Aligarh.
77. Our Tata Silk Farm.
78. Women winding silk.
79. Criminal boy with raw silk and silk cloth made at our factory.
80. The devil dancer of 'The Light of India,' page 60, or 'Other Sheep,' page 75.
81. Cape Comrin: Hindu Shrine.
82. Bathing Pool attached to Shrine.
83. The Sea-shore.
84. An Indian Corps Cadet.
85. A Group of Officers.
86. One of the most successful Soul-winners.
87. Ensign and Beggar.
88. A one-legged, paralysed Buddhist.
89. A Buddhist Priest.
90. Three Ceylonese Sergeants.
91. Salvation Army Graves.

1914 Salvation Army Lantern slide catalogue

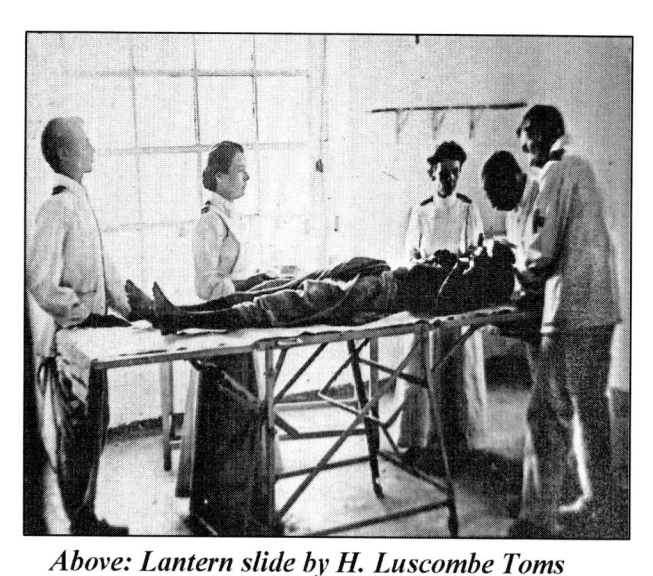

THE SALVATION ARMY AND THE CINEMATOGRAPH 1897 - 1929

Above: Lantern slide by H. Luscombe Toms

Left: Japanese looking at photographs of Bramwell and William Booth

to Comm. Yamamuro. Yamamuro had written an article for "All The World" in November 1926 relating to a conference which had taken place in Tokyo on 'brothels'. The Brothel Keepers convention had been held at the Ichimura Theatre in Shitaya, and Yamamuro had asked permission to address the conference but this had been refused. Instead he gave an interview to 'The Japan Advertiser' stating that in Japan there were 11,000 brothel houses and that brothels were treated like any other business even though, as Yamamuro claimed money was paid to the relatives of the women they hired, condemning them to a life of slavery. He had been fighting the licensing of prostitution since 1899.

Bramwell Booth arrived at Yokahama on 'The Empress of Canada'. Two thousand Salvationists carrying lanterns greeted him at Hibaya Park. Three thousand students were present for his appearance at the Auditorium in Keio University. He also visited the S.A. sanatorium as well as meeting the Japanese Prime Minister, Reijiro Wakatsuki.

Bramwell Booth's visit to Japan 1926. He is seated in the middle, front row. His son, Bernard, is standing at the far right-hand side.

THE SALVATION ARMY AND THE CINEMATOGRAPH 1897 - 1929

Above: 'Trouble ... Go where? ... Find SA Officers' From 'The Deliverer' December 1909

Centre: A Salvation Army willow pattern collection plate

At Tokyo, he met the Crown Prince at Alasaka Palace and received 3,000 yen from the Emperor and Empress. He also went to visit the poor and elderly at the Tokyo Civic Workhouse. Bramwell held a three-day conference with S.A. Officers from all over Japan.

At Sendai, the educational centre of the north of Japan, Bramwell held a meeting at Kokkaido Hall, including the Governor of Miyagi Prefecture, and the President of the Tohoku Imperial University as speakers. He held further meetings at Kyoto and Nagoya. During his 10 day visit a number of film records were taken of these events, some of which survive at the BFI. As records of the events, I think this series of films are visually the least interesting of the S.A. film collection

On his return to Britain, a welcome reception was held for Bramwell at the Royal Albert Hall where a number of these films were shown, with his son, Bernard, as lecturer. It was Bernard, who later wrote the script for 'William Booth, God's Soldier'.

In April 1930 Lt. Col. R.B. Chapman of Int. H.Q. advised the newly opened training H.Q. at Denmark Hill that he would loan them a Cinematograph projector and some films which could be used for training purposes for the S.A. Cadet Officers. He proposed the following nine titles:-

1) The Founder in Palestine.

1) The Founder's Funeral.

2) Star Lake Fresh Air Camp, USA.

3) Swedish Scout Camp.

4) Swedish Congress Meetings.

5) Stone Laying at the William Booth Memorial Training College.

6) Salvation Army Leper Colony Work.

7) General Booth in Japan.

8) A seven-reel (6,500 ft.) film of the Army's Work in India.

On the 26th August 1930 J. Arthur Morgan, the S.A. secretary for Education, advised Col. Knott of the Training College, that permission had been approved for a showing of 'India's Coral Strand' on September 1st.

General Bramwell Booth's meeting at Osaka in Japan. Illustration by Japanese S.A. Officer

POSTSCRIPT

In 1929 Maurice Elvey made a feature film entitled 'High Treason' which was based on a novel written by Pemberton Billings. The film was made in both silent and sound versions. Film technologies were changing – the Silent Cinematograph was on its last legs.

'High Treason' concerned the leader of a world peace movement trying to stop a war between the two continents of the East and West. The daughter of the leader of the peace movement falls in love with the son of the leader of the pro-war continent. The figure and the character of the leader of the peace movement, played by Humbertson Wright, bears close resemblance to Bramwell Booth, (who had just been ousted as the S.A.'s 'General'). In order to save world peace, the leader of the peace movement shoots and kills the leader of the war faction, and is then sentenced to death, a sentence which he accepts as being just.

In 1929, British Pathe filmed the S.A. High Council at Sunbury in Surrey, where they elected the successor to Bramwell Booth. Later that year, on June 24th, they filmed the lying-in-state of Bramwell at Clapton and on June 27th, his funeral at Abney Park.

Henry Howse, who had been instrumental in starting both the Cinematograph and the Lantern department of the S.A., seems to have disappeared off the radar following his visit to the Holy Land with William Booth in 1905. He became a travelling Cinematographer but did not eschew his S.A. background completely. The BFI holds a film entitled 'The Third Christmas' which was made by the Edison Film Company in the USA in 1913. At the beginning of the film there is an imprimatur of the S.A. which states that the film has been issued by the authority of General Booth and photographed by Henry Howse F.R.G.S.

The story was written by James Oppenheim and this 'film within a film' concerns a woman, who in order to make a living, becomes a film actress – the moral being that what she is doing is not intrinsically evil.

In 2004, an article appeared in the 'Salvationist' by Margaret Hammond which referred to her grandfather, Henry Howse. She stated that her mother, Mabel, (MacFarlane) had starred in a number of films which Henry had made. She recalled that her mother's favourite film was 'The Drunkard's Daughter' in which Mabel went to a saloon, threw open the swinging doors and begged her drunken father to return home. Margaret Hammond also stated that before her parents emigrated from England to Canada in 1924, they burned several reels of film which the S.A. H.Q. did not want.

Cinematograph presentation at the Slavation Army Citadel in Tottenham in 1906

THE SALVATION ARMY AND THE CINEMATOGRAPH 1897 - 1929

"ONE MOMENT, PLEASE, WHILE WE CHANGE REELS"

ADDENDUM
Selected films from the Salvation Army's 1906 Catalogue

A Salvation Army Officer's Funeral.

A Peep through 'The War Cry'.

Scenes in the Slums.

On Mile-End Waste, East London.

A Thrilling Rescue from the River.

March Past of Old Women at the Farm Colony, Hadleigh.

Innocent Recreation at the Farm Colony, Hadleigh – swinging.

The Social Workshop.

Salvation Army Printing Works.

The Staff Band at Manchester.

Cadets at Clapton.

Parkhead Juniors' Hoop-Drill.

The Matchseller and Ice-cream.

Feeding the Poor.

Parkhead Drill with Hoops and Tambourines – free Gymnasium.

Slum Open-air.

Farm Colony.

Cadet's Salute.

Seen in the Camera.

Saved by a Lie – the Story of a Crime and what the Salvation Army can do.

   Scene 1 – Set in 'The Green Man' – drunk attacks woman.

   Scene 2 – At Home – Drunk kicks wife – police arrive.

   Scene 3 – Hospital – she dies, exonerating drunk husband.

   Scene 4 – Husband standing over grave – with Capt. in S.A.

Children of the Slums – a day in the country by means of the Fresh-Air Fund of 'The Daily Express' and the Salvation Army.

"Hundreds of poor children are taken for a day in the country every summer. In this picture we see the start of a great number of urchins from their sombre alley for the more congenial surroundings of the country lanes and green fields, which they have never seen before.

Once in the country the promoters of these outings set themselves to work to provide sport and amusement for all their charges, and to those persons who have contributed a few coppers to this excellent cause, the look of intense pleasure on the faces of the little mites will be a true source of delight, and as one takes a look around the assembling ground, and listens to the happy shouts of the children, one is pleased with the excellent arrangements and the care bestowed upon each child. Motor rides, cricket matches, tug-o'-war, cake-walks, and all the harmless games are indulged in with a zest which defies description and the fine fresh air is enjoyed beyond measure. 'Feeding-time is a sight seldom seen'.

It is here that the eyes of the children are brightest and their faces become intensely eager as the substantial cakes are handed round, to which, it is unnecessary to add, full and complete justice is done. The Army takes thousands of children out every summer."

A Hindoo Sacrifice. – Young goats beheaded as a sacrifice – 'contrast this with the growing army of happy Indians saved from Heathen Darkness and worshipping the true and living God.'

Cinematograph Performances by the Salvation Army in India and Ceylon 1906-1919

References (years) from *India's War Cry*

Ahmedabad – 1906/07, 1908, 1913, 1915, 1916.

Ahmednagar – 1906/07, 1909, 1916.

Amritsar – 1906/07, 1909.

Anand – 1906/07, 1909, 1911, 1913, 1915.

Bangalore – 1911, 1915.

Bareilly – 1908, 1909, 1913, 1917.

Baptala – 1910, 1913.

Bartola - 1912

Batala – 1906/07, 1916.

Bettiah Settlement – 1913.

Bombay – 1906/07, 1911, 1913.

Calcutta – 1906/07, 1909, 1911, 1912, 1915.

Cawnpore – 1914.

Changa Manga – 1913, 1917.

Chautawa Settlement – 1913.

Colombo – 1911, 1913.

Danepur Settlement – 1913.

Dohad – 1906/07.

Ellore – 1906/07.

Fatepur – 1912.

Ghoton – 1909.

Gorakhpur – 1909, 1910, 1912.

Gudiwada – 1913.

Gujarat – 1911, 1913, 1915.

Gurdaspur – 1918.

Hewadiwela – 1910, 1911.

Jaffna – 1906/07, 1909.

Jiruvella – 1909/10

Jutogh – 1910.

Kandy – 1909, 1910.

Karampur – 1911.

Khanewal – 1918.

Kot Mokhal – 1913.

Kottarakarai – 1919.

Kottayam – 1913.

Lahore – 1906/07, 1909, 1911, 1912, 1913, 1918.

Lucknow – 1909, 1910.

Lyallpur – 1917.

Madras – 1906/07, 1909, 1911, 1913, 1915, 1917.

Maharashtra – 1909.

Mavelkurai – 1910.

Moradabad – 1906/07, 1908, 1910, 1913, 1917, 1918.

Moratuwa – 1910, 1911.

Muktipur Farm Colony – 1906/07, 1913.

Nagercoil – 1906/07, 1909, 1916, 1917.

Nellore – 1913.

Nowshera – 1914.

Palamcotta – 1909.

Para Chinar – 1910

Peyodro – 1909.

Poona – 1909, 1911, 1915, 1916.

Rawalpindi – 1910.

Rura – 1913.

Shantinagar – 1918.

Shiole – 1908.

Simla – 1908, 1910, 1911, 1912, 1913, 1915, 1917, 1918, 1919.

Talampitiya – 1913.

Tamasha – 1912.

Tiruvalla – 1910, 1913, 1916.

Travancore – 1910, 1911, 1913, 1919.

Trivandrum – 1906/07, 1909, 1910, 1911, 1913, 1916, 1917, 1919.

Undhera – 1908.

Vaso – 1908.

Wanowrie – 1911.

Venues for the 1926/27 Cinematograph Tour in Britain

A) September to December 1926 (Public Halls)

Folkestone Town Hall

Chatham Town Hall

Dover Town Hall

Pump Room, Tunbridge Wells

Dome, Brighton

Corn Exchange, Maidstone

Forester's Hall, Canterbury

Forester's Hall, Margate

Colchester

St. Albans

Wykeham Hall, Romford

Town Hall, High Wycombe

Devonshire Park, Eastbourne

Connaught Hall, Worthing

Southsea I (S. A. venue)

South Parade Pier, Portsmouth

Coliseum, Southampton

Victoria Hall, Salisbury

Winter Gardens, Bournemouth

Alexandra Hall, Newton Abbot

Guildhall, Plymouth

Barnfield Hall, Exeter

B) February to March 1927 (S. A. Halls)

Brightlingsea

Colchester

Clacton-on-Sea

Ipswich I

Hadleigh

Sudbury

Bury St. Edmunds

Upper Clapton

Huddersfield

Heckmondwike

Halifax

Bradford

Long Eaton

Derby

Ilkeston

Mansfield

Nottingham

Redhill

Tonbridge

Bexhill

Hastings I

Hove

Portslade

Silent Films from the Pathe & Movietone Archive

PATHE ARCHIVES

1) 18th March 1913 - Death of Adj. Kate Lee (aka 'The Angel Adjutant')

2) 1914 - Salvation Army Congress

3) 1914 - Salvation Army Procession

4) 9th July 1925 - Salvation Army's Jubilee

5) 1929 - Salvation Army High Council

6) 24th June 1929 - Lying-in-state of General Booth

7) 27th June 1929 - Passing of a Great Leader

MOVIETONE ARCHIVE

1) 1912 - Death of Sir William Booth (catalogued as 'Sir' incorrectly)

Main Salvation Army Ranks up to 1930

Cadet

Lieutenant (Lt.)

Captain (Capt.)

Ensign (Ens.)

Adjutant (Adj.)

Staff Captain

Major (Mjr.)

Brigadier (Brig.)

Lieutenant Colonel (Lt. Col.)

Colonel (Col.)

Commissioner (Comm.)

Chief of Staff (CoS.)

General (Gen.)

THE SALVATION ARMY INTERNATIONAL CONGRESS 1904. CELEBRATION AT THE CRYSTAL PALACE. TUESDAY, JULY 5TH

Main Sources

(References mainly between the dates 1890-1929)

All the World

Assurance

Australia's First Film - Chris Long and Clive Lowry (in Cinema Papers 1997/98)

The Bandsman and Songster

The Bioscope (1909)

The Booth-Tucker Family Papers

The British Film Catalogue - Denis Gifford

The British Salvation Army, The British Early film Industry etc. - Dean Rapp

(in 20th Century British History. Vol 7 No. 2 (1996))

The Call of the Jackals - W. Bramwell Baird (unpublished)

Catherine Bramwell-Booth Papers (including Bernard Booth)

Cinematograph Film catalogue (1906)

Cinematograph Department File

Consul Booth-Tucker - a sketch by Comm. Booth-Tucker (1907)

The Cox Family Papers

The Deliverer

Events Diary of Bramwell Booth

Federation Films - compiled by Chris Long (1991)

Feeding and Entertaining the Poor - Karen Eifler (in Kintop 3)

The Field Officer

He Was There - F. Hayter Cox

India's Nomads - John Lancaster (National Geographic) (February 2010)

India's War Cry (later 'The War Cry, India')

The Lantern Slide Catalogue (1914)

The Lantern Slide Collection at the Salvation Army Heritage Centre

The Local Officer

London Evening News (1920)

Melbourne Report (July 1997) (Faith, Federation and Film by Jan Chandler)

The Musician

The Musical Salvationist

Muktifauj or Forty Years with the Salvation Army in India and Ceylon by F. Booth-Tucker (1927)

My Fifty Eight Years by Comm. Parker (1943)

New Light in Limelight - The Salvation Army and the Film Industry 1890-1910 by Glen Hopper (1978)

The Officer

Optical Lantern and Cinematograph Journal 1907

Orders and Regulations for Officers

The Romance of a Motor Mission - W. P. Ryan

The Salvationist (2004)

Salvation Army Year Book

Salvation Army Trade Journal

Salvation Army Hand Book

The Social Awakening in London - Robert A. Woods (Scribner's Magazine 1892)

The Social Gazette

Stage and Cinema (1917)

Sundays and Holydays - Tony Fletcher (in Networks of Entertainment. Early Film Distribution 1895-1915)

Under the Colours

The War Cry

William Booth, God's Soldier - Script by H. Bernard Booth

The Young Soldier

The Y. P. (Young People)